MBE OUTLINE
FEDERAL CIVIL PROCEDURE

Federal Civil Procedure Outline for
the Multistate Bar Examination

*AmeriBar offers comprehensive bar review courses for 38 jurisdictions.
Visit ameribar.com for more information.*

AmeriBar
Phone (800) 529-2651 • Fax (800) 529-2652

MBE OUTLINE - FEDERAL CIVIL PROCEDURE

ISBN 1-50240-383-8

AMERIBAR BAR REVIEW

Multistate Bar Examination Preparation Course

CIVIL PROCEDURE

TABLE OF CONTENTS

CIVIL PROCEDURE

Civil procedure in federal courts is governed by the Federal Rules of Civil Procedure ("Rules").

I.   JURISDICTION AND VENUE

Jurisdiction is defined as the authority to hear a case and render a binding judgment. In order to decide a case, a federal court must possess subject matter jurisdiction over the dispute, and personal jurisdiction over the parties.

Venue is defined as the location in which a judicial proceeding takes place.

A.   Federal Subject-Matter Jurisdiction

A federal court can only decide a case if it has subject-matter jurisdiction over the case. Subject-matter jurisdiction refers to whether a court has the power to decide the kind of controversy involved in a case. Subject-matter jurisdiction cannot be consented to or waived by the parties. A party can challenge the existence of subject-matter jurisdiction at any time in the case, even on appeal.

Article III of the United States Constitution creates the Supreme Court of the United States. Articles I and III give the United States Congress the authority to establish lower federal tribunals. Congress has created a number of lower federal courts, including 13 circuit courts, and 91 district courts. The lower federal courts are tribunals of limited jurisdiction. For a controversy to come within the subject-matter jurisdiction of a federal court, it must satisfy one of several alternative jurisdiction requirements.

For bar exam purposes, a federal district court possesses subject-matter jurisdiction over two types of disputes: 1) federal questions; and 2) claims with diversity of citizenship.

★★★★   1)   FEDERAL QUESTION JURISDICTION

Congress has conferred upon federal courts, the jurisdiction to decide federal questions. 28 U.S.C. § 1331. A federal district court possesses limited original jurisdiction over a case arising under the United States Constitution, federal statutory or common law, and federal treaties. Article III requires that an actual "case or controversy" exist between the parties. A "case or controversy" involves a federal question only when a plaintiff's complaint states a claim or cause of action that involves federal law.

★★   a)   Well-Pleaded Complaint Rule

Federal question analysis is governed by the Well-Pleaded Complaint Rule. Under this rule, federal jurisdiction exists when a federal question is presented on the face of a plaintiff's properly pleaded complaint. A federal question is "presented" when the complaint invokes any type of federal law as the primary basis for relief.

(1)   Plaintiff is Master of Claim

The Well-Pleaded Complaint Rule makes a plaintiff the master of the claim. The plaintiff must affirmatively invoke federal subject-matter jurisdiction by pleading a federal-law claim within the complaint. A federal court does not have federal question subject-matter jurisdiction over a case based on state law that could also support a federal claim. Therefore, a plaintiff can avoid federal question jurisdiction by relying exclusively on state law to present a claim.

(2)   Federal Defense Insufficient

Under the Well-Pleaded Complaint Rule, a federal court lacks original jurisdiction over a case in which a plaintiff's complaint presents a state-law cause of action, but also asserts that: 1) federal law deprives a defendant of a defense that the defendant might raise (e.g., federal immunity); or 2) a federal defense that a defendant may raise is not sufficient to defeat a claim of the complaint.

★★★★   2)   <u>DIVERSITY OF CITIZENSHIP JURISDICTION</u>

In addition to jurisdiction over federal questions, federal district courts possess original jurisdiction over cases between parties of diverse state citizenship, if the claims of a complaint satisfy the jurisdictional amount in controversy requirement. The citizenship of the litigants, rather than the topic of the underlying controversy, defines the diversity jurisdiction.

Diversity subject-matter jurisdiction exists if: 1) the opposing parties are citizens of different states; and 2) the amount in controversy exceeds $75,000, exclusive of interests and costs.

★★★★   a)   Complete Diversity of Citizenship

Complete diversity of citizenship must exist between the parties on each side of a case. All of the plaintiffs must be citizens from different states than all of the defendants. Complete diversity means that there is no diversity jurisdiction when any party on one side of a dispute is a citizen of the same state as any party on the opposing side of the dispute.

★★   (1)   Determination of Citizenship

Citizenship is determined as of the time the action is commenced.

(a)   Individuals

In the context of diversity jurisdiction, citizenship is equivalent to domicile. A person is a citizen of the state in which she is domiciled. See the discussion of domicile in the section on personal jurisdiction for a detailed analysis.

(i)   Executor

For diversity purposes, when an executor of a decedent's estate is a defendant, the executor is "deemed to be a citizen only of the same state as the decedent" when the executor represents the decedent in litigation. 28 U.S.C. § 1332(c)(2).

(b)   Corporations

When analyzing diversity jurisdiction, a corporation may possess citizenship in two states. Here, the word "state" means the states of the United States and foreign states (i.e., nations).

(i)   State of Incorporation

A corporation is a citizen of its state of incorporation.

(ii)   Principal Place of Business

A corporation is also a citizen of the state in which it has its principal place of business. A corporation can have only one principal place of business. The principal place of business refers to the place where a corporation's officers direct, control, and coordinate the corporation's activities. It has been referred to as the "nerve center" of the corporation. It is normally the place where the corporation maintains its headquarters. However, the corporate headquarters will not be considered the principal place of business if it is not the actual center of direction, control, and coordination (e.g., if it is simply an office where the corporation holds its board meetings).

★★★★   b)   Amount in Controversy

(1)   Plaintiff must Demand Required Amount

A party can invoke diversity jurisdiction only if the amount in controversy exceeds $75,000, exclusive of interest and costs. If the amount in controversy is $75,000 or less, diversity jurisdiction does not exist. It does not matter if the party actually recovers $75,000 or more. So long as the sum that is demanded by a plaintiff in the complaint satisfies the jurisdictional amount, it will be accepted, unless it appears to a legal certainty that the claim is really for less than the jurisdictional amount.

(2)   Aggregation of Claims

If a plaintiff possesses two unrelated claims, which total over $75,000, against a single defendant, a plaintiff may sue in federal court because the aggregate exceeds $75,000. However, if two different plaintiffs each possess a claim that does not exceed $75,000, against one defendant, they cannot aggregate the claims, regardless of how similar the claims are. A plaintiff may aggregate claims against multiple defendants if they are joint tortfeasors under one claim.

(3)   Counterclaims

A counterclaim is a claim made by a defendant against a plaintiff. It may or may not arise from the same transaction or occurrence giving rise to the plaintiff's claim.

(a) Compulsory

If a counterclaim is compulsory (i.e., arising from same transaction or occurrence), then it will fall within the jurisdiction of the court and may be heard regardless of the amount in controversy. For example, if a defendant's compulsory counterclaim is in the amount of $15,000, then the defendant may assert it, if the plaintiff's claim exceeds $75,000.

(b) Permissive

If a counterclaim is permissive (i.e., not arising from the same transaction or occurrence), then it must possess an independent jurisdictional basis for federal jurisdiction. A permissive counterclaim must independently fulfill the jurisdictional amount requirement. In order to assert a counterclaim that is unrelated to the same transaction or occurrence, the amount of the defendant's claim must exceed $75,000.

(4) Injunctive Relief

The amount of a claim for an injunction is valued by either the amount that it will benefit a plaintiff, or by the cost that a defendant will incur to comply with it. This outline addresses injunctions separately.

(5) Domestic Relations Exception

A federal court will decline jurisdiction over a case involving the issuance of a divorce, alimony, or a child custody decree.

★★   3) <u>SUPPLEMENTAL JURISDICTION</u>

Subject-matter jurisdiction in a federal district court is generally limited to those types of controversies that are specifically enumerated in the United States Constitution and that Congress has authorized those courts to exercise. A federal court may exercise jurisdiction over certain claims (not cases or controversies) when those claims are properly joined in a single lawsuit with a distinct cause of action that is jurisdictionally sufficient.

At common law, jurisdiction over these claims was classified as pendent or ancillary jurisdiction. Congress codified those concepts under the doctrine of *supplemental jurisdiction*. 28 U.S.C. § 1367. Under the doctrine of supplemental jurisdiction, certain new parties and new claims may be added to a case without satisfying an independent subject-matter jurisdiction test. Thus, certain claims can, in effect, be added to the heart of a controversy under certain circumstances.

a) General Rule Includes Claims Related to Original Claims

In a civil action in which a district court has original jurisdiction, the district court also has supplemental jurisdiction over all other claims that are so related to claims in the action within such original jurisdiction that they form part of the same case or controversy. 28 U.S.C. §

1367(a). Two claims have the requisite connection if they "derive from a common nucleus of operative fact."

b)   Rule 14 Exception (Impleader)

Congress created a notable statutory exception to the general rule of supplemental jurisdiction. Supplemental jurisdiction does not extend to "claims by plaintiffs against persons made parties under Rule 14." 28 U.S.C. § 1367(b). Rule 14, further addressed in the Joinder portion of this outline, permits a party to bring a third-party complaint. When a party brings a third-party complaint against another entity, supplemental jurisdiction is unavailable. Under these circumstances, the claim must possess a satisfactory independent basis for subject-matter jurisdiction.

★★   4)   REMOVAL FROM STATE COURT TO FEDERAL COURT

Removal is the process of moving a case filed in a state court to a federal court.

★★   a)   Removal Requirements

Under certain circumstances, a case filed in a state court can be moved to a federal court. Only a defendant may remove a case to federal court. Additionally, the defendant cannot be a resident of the forum state (applicable only in potential diversity jurisdiction cases).

A case that is originally filed in a state court may be removed to a federal court if:

- the case could have been filed in a federal court (federal subject-matter jurisdiction exists);
- all defendants agree to remove the case; and
- the grounds for removal are included in at least one claim of a plaintiff (i.e., the grounds cannot be based on an affirmative defense or a counterclaim).

(1)   Fraudulent Joinder

If the plaintiff fraudulently joins a party to destroy diversity in order to prevent removal, a defendant may remove the case if he would have been able to remove the case absent the fraudulent joinder. In order to determine whether joinder is fraudulent for removal purposes, a federal court will inquire whether there is absolutely no chance that the cause of action against the purported defendant will succeed. If the plaintiff has no chance to succeed, then the court may find fraudulent joinder.

(2)   Preventing Removal

A plaintiff may prevent a defendant from removing a case by:

- not raising a federal claim; or
- not joining a party of diverse citizenship, and

- not pleading damages sufficient to allow removal (i.e., possibly requesting a lesser amount of damages than the amount in controversy)

★★   b)   Removal Procedure

In order to remove a case, a defendant files a notice of removal containing a short and plain statement of the grounds for removal, together with a copy of all process, pleadings, and orders served upon the defendant(s) in the action. The determination of which federal district court is proper is discussed under the topic of Venue.

            (1)   Removal is Automatic

A defendant is not required to file a motion to remove a case. Removal is automatic.

            (2)   Timing

A defendant must seek removal within 30 days from when: 1) the plaintiff serves a complaint; or 2) the case otherwise became removable (e.g., through adding a removable claim). However, a case that would be grounded in diversity is not removable more than one year from the date of the commencement of the action. But note, if the plaintiff has acted in bad faith (e.g., manipulates the timing of the case) to avoid removal on this ground, then the defendant(s) will be permitted to remove the case after this deadline.

★   c)   Motion to Remand

Once a case is removed to a federal court, a party may move to remand the case back to state court. The case may be remanded back to state court if the removal was improper.

            (1)   Timing

A party must move for remand with the federal court within 30 days from being served with a removal notice.

            (2)   Remand of Limited Claims

When a case removed to a federal court includes claims that fall outside the federal court's original and supplemental jurisdiction, the court must remand those non-jurisdictionally sufficient claims back to the state court.

            (3)   Not Appealable

If a federal court grants a motion for remand on the basis that the court lacks jurisdiction, the party who sought removal cannot appeal the determination.

★★   d)   Effect on Timing

            (1)   Time to Answer

In a removed action in which the defendant has not answered, the defendant must answer and/or present defenses within (the longer period of):

- 21 days after the receipt of a copy of the complaint or summons; or
- within 7 days after the filing of the notice for removal.

Receipt of a copy of the complaint need not be through service of process. If the defendant received a copy through another method, the time will run from such receipt, despite the fact that plaintiff has not served the complaint.

(2) Jury Demand

A party entitled to trial by jury must serve a demand within 14 days after the notice of removal is filed if the party is the removing party, or if not the moving party, within 14 days after service on the party of the notice of removal. A party who, prior to removal, made an express demand for trial by jury in accordance with state law, need not make a demand for a jury trial after removal.

★★★ B. Personal Jurisdiction

A federal court must possess personal jurisdiction over the parties in a dispute.

1) BASES OF PERSONAL JURISDICTION
There are several different grounds for a federal court to obtain personal jurisdiction over a party.

a) Grounds for Personal Jurisdiction

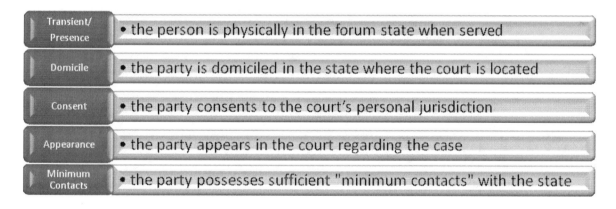

Transient/Presence	• the person is physically in the forum state when served
Domicile	• the party is domiciled in the state where the court is located
Consent	• the party consents to the court's personal jurisdiction
Appearance	• the party appears in the court regarding the case
Minimum Contacts	• the party possesses sufficient "minimum contacts" with the state

★   (1) Transient (Presence)

A court has jurisdiction over a party when the party is served with process within the forum state (the state where the court is located). A state is presumed to possess limited legal authority over all of the people who are found within its borders. If a person is served with legal process while present in a state, any length of stay therein, no matter how brief, is sufficient to establish transient jurisdiction in the state. In one case, personal jurisdiction was established over a defendant after service of process upon the defendant occurred in an airplane while it was flying over the forum state. *Grace v. MacArthur,* 170 F. Supp 442 (E.D. Ark. 1959). Note that service which is procured by fraudulently luring a defendant into the forum state will not be upheld as valid to provide personal jurisdiction.

★   (2)   Domicile

A person who possesses a domicile in a state is subject to a lawsuit in that forum state regarding a dispute that originated anywhere in the world.

A state is a person's domicile if the person possesses: 1) a physical presence in the state (i.e., residency); and 2) the person possesses an intent to reside there indefinitely (*First Restatement*), or to make it his home for the time at least (*Second Restatement*). A person can have many residences, but only one domicile.

(a)   Objective Test

A court uses an objective test to determine domicile. A court examines property and tax records, registrations, and other relevant documents, to determine if a state is a person's domicile.

(b)   Change of Domicile

A change of domicile may be accomplished when a person changes her place of residency to a new location with an intention to remain there, and while regarding it as the person's home. Friedenthal, Kane and Miller, *Civil Procedure* 31 (1996).

(c)   Forum State Rule Governs Domicile

Due to the relative uniformity with which the issue of domicile is treated throughout the United States, the question of which rule applies to determine domicile is usually insignificant. Occasionally, however, a local rule may alter the analysis of domicile. Generally, each jurisdiction applies its own rules regarding domicile when that issue arises in a case.

(3)   Consent

A party may consent to a court's personal jurisdiction. For example, a party may sign a contract containing a clause agreeing to personal jurisdiction in a particular state. Such a clause usually provides that the parties agree to be subject to a particular court's jurisdiction. Traditionally, a court would not enforce such a clause if the parties to the contract possessed a disparate level of bargaining power. Today, however, although such a clause could potentially be inherently unfair to a party, it would probably be enforced in the absence of fraud or duress, even if it was contained in a standard form agreement. *Carnival Cruise Lines, Inc. v. Shute,* 499 U.S. 585 (1991). This topic is further discussed under the subtopic of "Limitations on Personal Jurisdiction."

(4)   Appearance

Traditionally, a party to a lawsuit who voluntarily appeared in a court (in which a plaintiff filed a lawsuit), without making an objection to the court's personal jurisdiction over the party, was considered to have voluntarily submitted to the court's jurisdiction. Centuries ago, that rule had the effect of eliminating a party's right to directly attack the court's jurisdiction. If a party appeared in a court to attack the court's personal jurisdiction, then the party would have been considered to have submitted to the court's jurisdiction. As a result, a party that neither attacked nor submitted to the court's jurisdiction, would have been subject to the entry of a default judgment. The defaulting party could only collaterally attack that judgment when a prevailing party sought to enforce it in the defaulting party's home state.

Today, in almost all jurisdictions, a party may object to, and directly attack, the jurisdiction of a court at the beginning of a case without submitting to the court's jurisdiction. However, if the objecting party also seeks *affirmative* relief from the court, the objection to jurisdiction is waived, and the attack fails.

★★★★   (5)   Minimum Contacts

For exam purposes, the most important type of personal jurisdiction determination will be to analyze the extent of a person's minimum contacts with a forum state. In other words, the most commonly tested basis for personal jurisdiction is if a person's contacts with a forum state are sufficient to reasonably require the person to defend a lawsuit that is filed in the forum state.

Even if no other basis for personal jurisdiction applies, a forum state will possess personal jurisdiction over a defendant if the defendant possesses minimum contacts with the forum state. *International Shoe Company v. Washington* provides the general rule that a person who has never been present in a state still may be subject to personal jurisdiction in the state if the person possesses:

- "sufficient minimum contacts" with that forum state,
★★★★ •   such that requiring the person to appear and defend in a court there would not
- "offend traditional notions of fair play and substantial justice."

Memorize this rule.

★★   (a)   General and Specific Jurisdiction

                 (i)   Continuous and Systematic

If a defendant's contact with the forum state is continuous and systematic, then the court has personal jurisdiction over the defendant in a case involving the defendant's activity in the state, and any other activity unrelated to the defendant's activity in the forum state. This type of jurisdiction is referred to as general jurisdiction. *Helicopteros Nacionales v. Hall,* 466 U.S. 408 (1984).

Generally, the owner of a website on the internet is not subject to personal jurisdiction everywhere, solely on the basis that the owner maintains the website that can be accessed everywhere. As a general proposition, the likelihood that the owner would be subject to personal jurisdiction may be proportionate to the extent to which the website is interactive. *Zippo Mfg. Co. v. Zippo Dot Com, Inc.*, 952 F. Supp. 1119 (W.D. Pa. 1997). Thus, such jurisdiction probably would not be supported merely on the basis of an entirely passive website. *Id.*

(ii)   Sporadic Activity

In order for sporadic activity in the forum state to justify the exercise of jurisdiction, the cause of action must be *related* to the defendant's activity in the forum state. In other words, sporadic activity may subject a defendant to personal jurisdiction *only if* the cause of action arises out of activity in the state. This type of jurisdiction is referred to as *specific jurisdiction*.

★★   (b)   Purposeful Availment

The exercise of personal jurisdiction is more likely if a party *purposefully avails* itself of the benefits of the forum state. For example, if a party advertises to a market in the state, the court would be more likely to exercise jurisdiction over the person.

In *Hanson v. Denckla*, the United States Supreme Court stated that:

> It is essential in each case that there be some act by which the defendant purposefully avails itself of the privilege of conducting activities within the forum state, thus invoking the benefits and protections of its laws.

★★   (c)   Stream of Commerce

If a defendant places a product into the "*stream of commerce*," giving rise to a claim against the defendant in a forum state's court, then when determining whether personal jurisdiction exists, the court may examine the *foreseeability* of the product's presence in the forum state.

(i)   Placing Product Into Stream of Commerce

In *World-Wide Volkswagen Corporation v. Woodson*, the plaintiffs were New York citizens who filed a tort action in an Oklahoma court to recover damages for the injuries that they suffered in an automobile accident in that forum state. Two defendants, a New York car dealer and a New York car distributor, challenged the forum court's personal jurisdiction over them. The United States Supreme Court determined that the Oklahoma court did not have personal jurisdiction over the New York defendants, finding that merely placing the automobile into the "stream of commerce" did not alone warrant personal jurisdiction over them. Rather, the Supreme Court concluded that:

> The foreseeability that is critical to due process analysis is not the mere likelihood that a product will find its way into the forum State. Rather, it is that the defendant's conduct and connection with the forum State are such that he should reasonably anticipate being haled into court there... It is foreseeable that purchasers of automobiles sold by [defendants] may take them to Oklahoma. But the mere unilateral activity of those who claim some relationship with a non-resident defendant cannot satisfy the requirement of contact with the forum State.

(ii)   Fair Play and Substantial Justice

In *Asahi Metal Industry Company v. Superior Court*, a Japanese manufacturer served as a primary supplier of tire valves to a tire-tube manufacturer in Taiwan. The Japanese manufacturer knew that some of the tire-tubes would be sold in California. The United States Supreme Court determined that a California court lacked personal jurisdiction over the Japanese manufacturer in the Taiwan manufacturer's indemnification action. The Supreme Court decided that an exercise of personal jurisdiction would offend the *traditional notions of fair play and substantial justice* because:

- the forum-state court would have to adjudicate an international case;
- the "alien defendant" would suffer a heavy burden to defend the case; and
- the state had a weak interest in providing a forum for non-citizens.

In line with *World-Wide Volkswagon*, in the main opinion, Justice O'Connor and three other Justices determined that merely placing the product in the "stream of commerce" did not suffice to find minimum contacts, even if it was foreseeable that the product would be marketed in the forum state. In a concurring opinion, Justice Brennan and three other Justices determined that such foreseeability sufficed to find minimum contacts.

(iii)   Courts' Split of Authority by Test Used

Some federal and state courts follow O'Connor's analytical test, and others follow Brennan's.

- O'Connor's "Foreseeability-Plus" Test

Under O'Connor's test, without a defendant doing anything more relative to a forum state, the defendant's awareness that its product would be marketed in the forum state does not suffice to establish minimum contacts. In order to find minimum contacts, the defendant also must purposefully direct acts toward the forum state indicating the defendant's *purpose or intent* to serve the forum state's market. Such acts include advertising in the forum state, marketing there through the defendant's sales agent, establishing ways to advise customers there, or designing the product for the market there. But the defendant's mere awareness that the "stream of commerce" will or may take the product into the forum state does not convert the defendant's mere act of putting the product in the stream into an act purposefully directed toward the forum state.

- Brennan's "Mere Foreseeability" Test

Under Brennan's test, a defendant's *awareness* that its product would be marketed in the forum state, *in and of itself,* suffices to find minimum contacts when the product causes injury there.

★★   (d)   Reasonableness

The overall question when conducting any minimum contacts analysis is whether the assertion of jurisdiction is *reasonable under the circumstances*. A court will examine whether the defendant should have reasonably anticipated being brought into court in the jurisdiction.

2)   <u>LIMITS ON EXERCISE OF PERSONAL JURISDICTION</u>

★

a)   Long-Arm Statute

Testing the existence of personal jurisdiction is generally a two prong analysis. A court must possess one of the grounds for personal jurisdiction. Additionally, the exercise of jurisdiction must satisfy the jurisdiction's long-arm statute.

A long-arm statute authorizes jurisdiction and out-of-state service on a defendant.

(1)   Maximum Scope

In many states, long-arm statutes generally authorize personal jurisdiction over, and service of process upon, out of state parties in a civil action on any basis that is consistent with the limits of the Due Process Clause of the United States Constitution. Therefore, if an action satisfies one of the tests set forth in the section above regarding personal jurisdiction, then the action will also satisfy the state's long-arm statute. These long-arm statutes are the most liberal in terms of their scope of reach outside of the forum state.

(2)   Specified Scope

The long-arm statutes in some states are more limited in their extent of permissible grounds for obtaining personal jurisdiction over, and service of process upon, out-of-state parties in a civil action. Those long-arm statutes provide that only specified activities constitute a contact with the forum state that would empower a court's exercise of personal jurisdiction. Usually the occurrence of only one contact with the forum state as a result of the activities will provide a basis for jurisdiction. Those long-arm statutes are more conservative in terms of their scope of reach outside of the forum state.

The types of activities that may subject a party to personal jurisdiction include, but are not necessarily limited to the:

- transaction of any business within the state;
- commission of a tort within the state;
- ownership, use, or possession of real estate in the state; and
- making of, or the performance of, any contract in the state.

For example, the United States Supreme Court held in *Burger King v. Rudzewicz* that a Florida court possessed personal jurisdiction over a Michigan franchisee based on a contract which indicated that the parties' relationship was established in Florida, and that Florida Law governed their contractual relationship. The Supreme Court ruled, however, that the existence of such a contract cannot, of itself, give rise to a non-forum state party's sufficient minimum contacts with the forum state. Rather, the Supreme Court sustained the personal jurisdiction on the following grounds that may be relevant to analyzing an exam issue:

- The parties engaged in a substantial and continuous business relationship;

- The non-forum state party received fair notice that it could be subject to personal jurisdiction in the forum state. That notice resulted from the contract's terms and the parties' course of dealings; and
- The non-forum state party was sophisticated and experienced in business and did not enter into the contract due to duress or economic disadvantage.

(3) Federal Courts

Although no general federal long-arm statute exists, Rule 4(k)(1)(A) authorizes a federal court to utilize the long-arm statue of the forum state in which it is are located. Consequently, the federal courts possess the same scope of personal jurisdiction as the forum state courts.

b) Traditional Limitations

(1) Choice of Forum by Agreement

The existence of a forum-selection clause in a contract will be a significant factor in a court's decision of whether to exercise jurisdiction over a party. The court must evaluate the fairness of the proposed exercise of jurisdiction in light of the forum-selection clause. Although that clause must be treated as a significant factor when a court evaluates jurisdiction, the Supreme Court has held that the existence of a forum-selection clause is not dispositive of the issue of jurisdiction.

As mentioned under the subtopic of "Consent" to personal jurisdiction, an inequality of bargaining power between the parties may warrant giving less effect to their contract's forum-selection clause. Similarly, litigating in its preordained forum may impose significant and unusual hardships on one of the parties. The questions for evaluating a forum-selection clause are: 1) Does the forum selected in the clause have some connection to the contract?; and 2) Has a party overreached by attempting to include the clause in the contract?

(2) Fraud, Force, and Privilege

Jurisdiction that is obtained by fraud or force is invalid. For example, if a plaintiff tricks or lures a defendant into coming into a forum state and serves the defendant with process while in that state, a court will lack jurisdiction over the defendant. Representatives of foreign sovereigns who are in a forum state on business are generally immune from service. People who are present in a forum state to address the needs of litigation there may not be subject to personal jurisdiction as a result of service of process upon them in that state.

c) Constitutional Limitations (due process)

Regardless of which type of long-arm statute is controlling in a particular case, a court's exercise of personal jurisdiction that exceeds the scope of personal jurisdiction which is allowed under the Due Process Clause of the United States Constitution would be unconstitutional and could result in an invalid and unenforceable judgment.

3) IN REM JURISDICTION

In rem jurisdiction is a court's jurisdiction over property that is located within the forum state. In a usual dispute that gives rise to *in personam* (i.e., personal) jurisdiction, two or more people attempt to adjudicate their rights *in relation to each other*.

When *in rem* jurisdiction is invoked, a court adjudicates the *entire world's rights in relation to a piece of property*. The property can be either real property (e.g., building or land) or personal property (e.g., decedent's estate). In an *in rem* proceeding, the court may exercise its power to determine the ownership of the property. An *in rem* judicial determination is binding with respect to all possible interest holders if reasonable notice of the proceeding was given.

4)   QUASI IN REM JURISDICTION

A *quasi in rem* action is different from an *in personam* action that determines the rights of parties to certain property that is at issue. A *quasi in rem* action is initiated when a plaintiff seizes property within a forum state by means of attachment or garnishment. Traditionally, the property seized is used as a pretext for a court to decide a case without possessing personal jurisdiction over a defendant. Although the court may decide issues in a case that are unrelated to the property, the amount of the judgment is limited to the value of the property that is seized. The judgment cannot be sued upon in any other court. The United States Supreme Court has severely limited, if not eliminated, classic *quasi in rem* jurisdiction absent the existence of some other adequate ground for personal jurisdiction.

★★   C.   Service of Process and Notice

1)   ISSUANCE

Upon or after filing the complaint, the plaintiff may present a summons to the clerk for its signature. If the summons is in proper form, the clerk must sign, seal, and issue it to the plaintiff for service on the defendant. The plaintiff is responsible for service of the summons and a copy of the complaint.

2)   PERSONAL SERVICE ON INDIVIDUAL

An individual may be served in any federal judicial district pursuant to the state law of the jurisdiction in which the defendant is found.

Alternatively, an individual defendant may be served in the following three manners:

- delivery in person;
- copy delivered to residence or usual place of abode with person of suitable age and discretion residing therein; or
- delivery to authorized agent.

An infant or incompetent person may be served only in a manner prescribed by the state in which the defendant is to be served.

a)   Service on Minor or Incompetent Persons

A minor or an incompetent person must be served by following state law provisions governing service on minors or incompetents in the state where service is made. A minor or an incompetent person outside of the country must be served according to the rules of service of the foreign nation, the foreign court, or as ordered by the federal court hearing the action.

3)   SERVICE ON CORPORATIONS

A corporation may be served in any federal judicial district pursuant to the state law of the jurisdiction in which the defendant is found.

Alternatively, service may be made by delivering a copy of the summons and complaint to an officer, a managing or general agent, or to any other agent authorized by appointment or by law to receive service of process.

4)   FOREIGN SERVICE

An individual or corporation may be served outside of any judicial district of the United States by any internationally agreed means of service that is reasonably calculated to give notice (e.g., Hague Convention on the Service Abroad of Judicial and Extrajudicial Documents).

If no such agreement applies, then the party may be served:

- under a method of service provided by the law of the nation of service,
- under a method of service provided by a foreign court aiding the action,
- by delivering a copy of the summons and complaint to the individual personally (if not prohibited by applicable foreign law),
- by using any form of mail that the clerk addresses and sends to the individual and that requires a signed receipt (if not prohibited by applicable foreign law), or
- by any means directed by the federal court if it is reasonably calculated to give notice.

5)   TIME FOR SERVICE

If a summons and complaint are not served on a defendant within 120 days after filing the complaint, and the party seeking service cannot show good cause, the action should be dismissed as to that defendant, without prejudice.

6)   WHO MAY SERVE

The summons and complaint may be served by:

- any citizen of the United States;
- who is over 18 years of age; and
- not a party.

A party may request that service be made by a U.S. Marshall, Deputy Marshall, or other appropriate official.

7)   WAIVER OF SERVICE

A person or entity subject to service that receives proper notice of an action has a duty to avoid unnecessary costs of serving the summons. Therefore, in order to avoid costs, a plaintiff may notify a defendant of the commencement of an action and request that the defendant waive the service of the summons. The notice and request *must be in writing* and addressed to the defendant. It must be dispatched by first class mail or other reliable means.

A waiver of service of process must:

- contain a copy of the complaint;
- inform the defendant of the consequences of compliance (waiver of defenses relating to service of process); and
- inform the defendant of the consequences of non-compliance with the request (e.g., additional costs).

The defendant is provided a reasonable time to return the waiver, which must be at least 30 days from the date on which the request is sent.

If a defendant located within the United States fails to comply with a proper request for waiver, a court will impose the costs subsequently incurred in effecting service on the defendant *unless good cause* for the failure to comply is shown.

A defendant that timely returns a waiver properly requested is not required to serve an answer to the complaint until 60 days after the date on which the request for waiver of service was sent.

8)   CONSTITUTIONAL REQUIREMENTS

A method of service of process cannot be employed if it would violate the United States Constitution. In order for a method of service to satisfy constitutional requirements, the method must be *reasonably calculated* to provide notice of the action and afford the defendant an opportunity to present objections.

a)   Notice and Opportunity to be Heard

Beyond the requirement that a court possess jurisdiction over a case, *constitutional due process* requires that a party to a lawsuit receive:

- notice of the case; and
- an opportunity to be heard in a court.

A judgment that is entered in an action in which a party did not receive notice or have an opportunity to be heard is invalid and unenforceable against the party.

(1)   Notice

Notice may be given by serving (i.e., delivering) the requisite legal papers upon a party in person, *even if* the service occurs outside of the court's scope of personal jurisdiction. The papers served on a party must be *reasonably calculated* to adequately inform the defending party of the nature of a cause of action that is asserted by the claiming party. The defending party must be provided with a reasonable time to respond and prepare a defense to the cause of action.

(2)   Opportunity to Be Heard

The concept of an opportunity to be heard arises from the common law notion that a person with a legitimate dispute is entitled to a have a proverbial *"day in court."* The concept is now included under the constitutional principle of *due process*. An opportunity to be heard means that the parties to a dispute are entitled to receive an *impartial* court hearing on their claims and defenses

D.   Venue, Forum Non Conveniens, and Transfer

★★★   1)   VENUE GENERALLY

The term venue refers to the location of the court hearing an action. Venue usually does not implicate the constitutionality of a court's exercise of authority to adjudicate a dispute. Venue rules concern the propriety of the location of the court in which proceedings are conducted. Venue rules are based on the location of the parties and legal questions at issue. Venue objections may be waived if not timely asserted.

★★★   a)   Federal Court

Whether a venue is proper depends upon two considerations:

- type or classification of each party (corporate v. individual); and
- circumstances.

(1)   Individual Parties

There are three factors which must be analyzed in order to determine appropriate venue for actions involving individuals. These factors apply to cases in which the subject-matter jurisdiction is based on either diversity of citizenship or a federal question.

(a)   Residence

Venue is proper in a judicial district where any defendant resides (i.e., is domiciled), if all defendants reside in the same state of the judicial district; or

(b)   Act or Property

Venue is proper in a judicial district in which a substantial part of the events or omissions giving rise to the claim occurred; or in which most of the property that is subject to the action is located.

(c)   No Other District -- "Fallback Venue"

Venue is proper in a judicial district in which any of the defendants are subject to personal jurisdiction in the action, if there is no district in which the action may otherwise be brought.

(2)   Corporate Parties

Different circumstances need to be considered when determining venue for corporations. 28 U.S.C. § 1391(d). For venue purposes, a defendant corporation is deemed to reside in any judicial district in which it is subject to personal jurisdiction at the time the action is commenced. *Id.* For the purpose of determining a court's personal jurisdiction, a defendant-corporation that resides in a state with more than one judicial district is considered to reside in any district within that state where the corporation has contacts sufficient to establish personal jurisdiction if that district were a separate state. *Id.* If no such district exists, the corporation will be deemed to reside in the district within which it has the most significant contacts. *Id.*

★   b)   Removal Venue

In cases removed to federal court from state court, venue is proper in the federal district in which the state court sits when the district court possesses original jurisdiction over the case. This special rule produces an anomalous result because it makes venue proper in a federal district in which the action could not have originally been brought if a plaintiff had initially filed a lawsuit in that improper venue. 28 U.S.C. § 1441(a).

c)   Improper Venue Dismissal

A defendant may move to dismiss an action on the basis that it was filed in an improper venue.

d)   Options Other than Dismissal for Improper Venue

A defendant may move to transfer venue or make a motion asserting the doctrine of *forum non conveniens.*

2)   FORUM NON CONVENIENS

The doctrine of *forum non conveniens* allows for the dismissal of a case despite the existence of proper venue, personal jurisdiction, and subject-matter jurisdiction if:

- another forum is more convenient; and
- the interests of justice would be served by litigating the case elsewhere.

Federal district courts now primarily analyze a *forum non conveniens* issue under a federal statute rather than applying the traditional doctrine. *Id.* In most cases, a federal district court would be able to transfer a case to another federal district court. Nonetheless, a federal district court may dismiss an action based on the doctrine if the only permissible alternative forums would be either a state court or a court of a foreign nation because the court would not possess the ability to transfer the case to another court system. The court could grant the dismissal without prejudice so that the court could hear the action if the other court system declines jurisdiction.

★★　　　　　3)　　　VENUE TRANSFER

A federal district court may transfer a civil action to any other federal district or division where the action might have been brought, or to any district or division to which all parties have consented.

a)　　General Grounds for Change of Venue

More than one venue may be a proper venue to hear a dispute. For example, both the Northern District of Florida and the Southern District of Florida may be proper venues to bring a certain action. A defendant may seek to change the initial venue that the plaintiff selected to a venue that the defendant prefers. A defendant may be entitled to a change or transfer of venue if the initial venue is improper, or if a subsequent venue would be more convenient to the parties and witnesses.

b)　　Motion for Change of Venue

A defendant may file a motion to transfer venue on the basis that the existing venue is inappropriate and another venue would be more appropriate. A federal court may, *sua sponte* (i.e., of its own will), make its own motion to transfer venue.

(1)　　Improper Venue

Generally, if a court orders a change of venue to remedy a plaintiff's improper selection of venue, then the case should be transferred to another court within that judicial system that possesses proper venue.

(2)　　More Convenient Venue

Even if a plaintiff files a lawsuit in a proper venue, that initial court possesses discretion to order a change of venue to a location that is more appropriate. In that event, if a defendant files a motion to transfer venue to a subsequent court in the same state, the initial court may, in its discretion, grant the motion to transfer venue after consideration of whether it would:

- increase the convenience of the parties and witnesses; and
- promote the interests of justice (e.g., location of evidence and judicial efficiency).

(3)   Where Case Might Have Been Brought

The governing statute permits venue transfer to a venue in which the case "might have been brought." The United States Supreme Court interpreted the phrase "might have been brought" in as limiting a federal district court's discretionary power to transfer a case to another venue where the plaintiff could have originally filed the lawsuit. Thus, both personal jurisdiction and venue must exist, and cannot have been waived.

c)   Consent to Change of Venue

(1)   Where Case Could Not Have Been Brought

A federal district court may transfer a case to *any* venue to which the parties have consented, *only if* that would increase the convenience of parties and witnesses and promote the interests of justice. In that event, the court may make a consent venue transfer despite the inability to have originally filed the case in the transfer venue. 28 U.S.C. § 1404(a).

II.   LAW APPLIED BY FEDERAL COURTS

A.   State Law in Federal Court

A federal court, hearing a case based on diversity jurisdiction, must apply the law of the state in which the court sits. 28 U.S.C. § 1652.

1)   TRADITIONAL APPROACH WHICH IS NOW REJECTED

The traditional rule, set forth in *Swift v. Tyson,* provided that a federal court only applied state law created by the state legislature. Therefore, a federal court applied the state constitution and statutes, but could disregard judicial decisions (state common law). The *Swift* rule created competing lines of federal and state common law regarding state law issues. This fostered an environment of forum shopping between federal and state courts.

★★   2)   *ERIE* DOCTRINE

The seminal *Erie* case rejected the rule in *Swift.* The *Erie* doctrine has two effects for exam purposes. First, state *common law* applies in federal diversity cases. Second, state choice-of-law rules apply in federal cases.

a)   State Common Law Applies in Federal Cases

Under *Erie,* a federal court cannot avoid state common law when it does not agree with a state court's conclusion on an issue of state law. As a general rule, *Erie* established that there is no federal common law for diversity cases. Consequently, when a federal court is hearing a case under its diversity jurisdiction, it must apply the same substantive law that would have been applied if the suit had been filed in a court of the state where the federal court is located. *Erie*

R.R. Co. v. Tompkins, 304 U.S. 64 (1938). The federal court is not free to make its own independent judgment, from a policy standpoint, of the better construction of an ambiguous statute. *Id.* Instead, the federal court must try to predict from available state case law how the state's highest court would likely interpret the statute.

b) Choice-of-Law Rules of Forum State

Under the *Erie* doctrine, in diversity cases, a federal court also uses the choice-of-law rules of the state in which the court sits to determine which state's substantive law governs. The principal reason for this application of *Erie* is to deter forum-shopping between federal and state courts in the same state, and thereby protect the integrity and uniformity of state law within its territory.

For example, suppose that a plaintiff files, in a California federal court, a negligence claim stemming from an accident in Nevada. Under California substantive negligence law, the plaintiff would prevail in the action, but under Nevada substantive law, the defendant would prevail. If the federal court applied the substantive law of California, the court would find for the plaintiff. However, suppose that a California *state* court would have used state choice-of-law rules to apply the law of Nevada to the case. A California federal court would arrive at a different decision than a California state court. *Erie* resolved this potential conflict by requiring the federal court to apply the choice-of-law rules of the forum state. Therefore, the California federal court in our example would apply the law of Nevada, and find for the defendant.

c) Effect of Venue Transfer

A transfer of a civil action initiated by a defendant in a federal case, under the federal venue transfer statute, does not alter the state rule that would have been adopted by the transferor court. *Van Dusen v. Barrack*, 376 U.S. 612 (1964). This rule applies even when the plaintiff institutes the transfer. *Ferens v. John Deere Co.,* 110 S. Ct. 1274 (1990).

★ **B.   Federal Common Law**

Federal common law refers to the law set forth by judges in federal court decisions.

1)   FEDERAL COMMON LAW OF FEDERAL LAW

Federal common law evolves from federal case law that construes or completes gaps in federal constitutional provisions, statutes, or treaties. Only federal common law of federal law may possess a preclusive effect. Some additional examples of federal common law topics include suits involving the federal government and its employees, suits between states, suits concerning foreign relations, and suits involving federal statutes.

a)   State Court Follows Federal Common Law

A state court must apply federal common law when deciding issues of federal law.

2)   NO FEDERAL COMMON LAW OF STATE LAW

As explained above, there is no federal common law of *state law matters*. As a result of the *Erie* doctrine, only state, not federal common law, has preclusive effect in federal diversity actions.

III.   PRE-TRIAL PROCEDURES

★★★   A.   Preliminary Injunctions and Temporary Restraining Orders

An injunction is a court order requiring a person to engage in, or cease engaging in, a specific action. For example, a court may enter an injunction requiring a party to sell a piece of property pursuant to a contract.

An injunction may be classified as mandatory or prohibitory. An injunction that compels an act, is a mandatory injunction. An injunction that forbids an act, is a prohibitory injunction.

1)   PERMANENT INJUNCTION AND DECLARATORY JUDGMENT

a)   Permanent Injunction

A party may seek a permanent injunction as the ultimate relief in a case. For example, if a plaintiff alleges that the defendant is violating a non-competition agreement, the plaintiff may seek an injunction prohibiting the defendant from violating the agreement. The entry of a *permanent* injunction would only be permissible after a full trial of the case on the merits. By contrast, a temporary injunction may be ordered after a preliminary hearing.

In order to obtain a permanent injunction, a party must establish that:

- the party will suffer *irreparable* injury unless an injunction is issued;
- the threatened injury outweighs any harm the proposed injunction may cause to the opposing party, and
- an injunction would not be adverse to the public interest.

b)   Declaratory Judgment

An action seeking a declaratory judgment may be instituted to seek the court's opinion regarding the parties' rights under the law or an instrument such as a contract. Essentially, the parties ask the court whether a certain action is prohibited before a contract is breached or a law is violated.

(1)   Scope of Declaratory Judgments

Any person interested under a deed, contract, or other writings or whose rights a law affects may have the court determine any question of construction or validity arising under the instrument or law and obtain a declaration of rights thereunder. The declaration may be either affirmative or negative in form and effect, and such declarations will have the force and effect of a final judgment. After analyzing the parties' dispute, the court renders an opinion declaring their respective rights without ordering relief.

2)   TYPES OF NON-PERMANENT INJUNCTIONS

Usually, a party cannot wait until a final determination for entry of a permanent injunction. Such a process may take months or even years. Therefore, a litigant may seek a temporary injunction for the time up until the final determination.

There are two types of non-permanent injunctions:

- temporary restraining orders (TROs); and
- preliminary injunctions.

The difference between the two concerns timing. A TRO is sought in emergency situations when notice to the other party is not feasible. A preliminary injunction is often sought after a TRO is set to expire.

★★   a)   Temporary Restraining Order

A court may issue a TRO on an *ex-parte* basis (i.e., without the other party present) when necessary to prevent *irreparable* injury. Fed. R. Civ. P. 65(b). Because notice to the other party may not be required, a TRO is an extraordinary remedy.

To obtain an *ex-parte* TRO, the moving party must meet three conditions:

         (1)   Conditions

         (a)   Irreparable Injury

In a verified complaint or by affidavit (under oath), the moving party must set out specific facts that show that immediate and irreparable injury will result to the moving party before the adverse party can be heard in opposition.

         (b)   Efforts Made

The moving party must certify to the court, in writing, the efforts made to give the notice and the reasons supporting the claim that notice should not be required.

         (c)   Security

The moving party must provide a bond to the court in such a sum as the court deems proper to compensate the adverse party in the event that the TRO is wrongfully entered.

         (2)   Duration

The Rules limit temporary restraining orders to 14 days absent good cause. Remember, the key characteristic of a TRO is that notice to the other party may not be required.

★★   b)   Preliminary Injunction

A preliminary injunction is an injunction entered, with notice to the opposing party, before a final determination of the case. Fed. R. Civ. P. 65(a). Generally speaking, the only practical difference between a TRO and a preliminary injunction is that a preliminary injunction is issued:

- *after* a moving party provides notice to a non-moving party; and
- *after* the non-moving party has an opportunity to be heard.

The purpose of a preliminary injunction is to maintain the *status quo* until the parties' claims can be investigated and adjudicated.

(1)   Notice

Unlike a TRO, a party seeking a preliminary injunction must provide reasonable notice to the opposing party.

(2)   Factors Courts Generally Examine

When determining whether to grant a preliminary injunction, a court may examine several factors.

(a)   Likelihood of Success on Merits

A court considering whether to enter a preliminary injunction may consider whether the moving party made a strong showing that it is likely to prevail on the merits.

(b)   Irreparable Injury

A court considering whether to enter a preliminary injunction may consider whether the moving party has shown that without such relief, it will suffer irreparable injury.

(c)   Harm to Others

A court considering whether to enter a preliminary injunction may consider whether the issuance of the injunction would substantially harm other interested parties.

(d)   Public Interest

A court considering whether to enter a preliminary injunction must conduct an examination of the public interest under the circumstances.

★★   B.   **Pleadings and Amended and Supplemental Pleadings**

1)   NOTICE PLEADING VERSUS PLAUSIBILITY PLEADING

Under the Federal Rules of Civil Procedure, "notice" pleading was traditionally required for stating a claim, under which a complaint merely had to provide the opposing party with notice of the nature of the claim. Currently, "plausibility" pleading is required for stating a claim, under which a complaint must now allege enough facts to state a plausible claim for relief. Plausibility is addressed in the discussion regarding motions to dismiss for failure to state a claim.

2) NATURE AND STYLE OF PLEADINGS

A pleading must be simple, concise, and direct.

a) Pleading may be Inconsistent or Alternative

A pleading may be inconsistent or alternative. A pleading should contain short and plain statements.

(1) Election of Remedies Doctrine Rejected

The Rules reject the common law "Election of Remedies" doctrine. Under the common law, a plaintiff was required to choose a method of recovery for harm. Once a method of recovery was selected, the plaintiff could not assert an alternative or inconsistent method of recovery.

b) Pleading Special Matters

Special matters must be plead with particularity. Special matters include fraud, mistake, judgments, and special damages.

c) Verification Not Required

Verification (oath or notarization) of pleadings is generally unnecessary unless required by statute or unless requesting equitable relief. Once a pleading is verified, responsive pleadings must also be made under oath.

3) TYPES OF PLEADINGS

Pleadings include the complaint, answer, answer to counterclaim, answer to cross-claim, third-party complaint, and third-party answer.

a) Complaint

A complaint is the legal pleading that a plaintiff files with a court clerk to initiate a lawsuit. The complaint sets out facts and legal claims (usually called causes of action). To complete the initial stage of a lawsuit, the complaint must be served on the defendant, who then has the opportunity to respond.

b) Answer

An answer is a pleading that challenges a plaintiff's right to the relief that is requested in a complaint. The answer must admit or deny the allegations that are set forth in a complaint. Alternatively, the answer may assert a defendant's lack of sufficient knowledge to admit or deny an allegation. If a defendant fails to deny, or address, an allegation in the complaint, the court may deem the allegation admitted.

(1) Time for Service

An answer must be served within 21 days after the service of the complaint.

(2) Affirmative Defenses

Affirmative defenses may be served concurrently with the answer. They must be short and specific. Any omitted defenses may be asserted in an amended pleading either as a matter of right or pursuant to the granting of a motion to amend the pleading.

★   (3) Counterclaims

An answer may contain a counterclaim. A counterclaim is a claim that is made by a defendant in a civil lawsuit against a plaintiff. It is generally served with the answer and the affirmative defenses within 21 days from the receipt of process. In essence, it is a counter-suit within a lawsuit. Counterclaims are either compulsory or permissive. See the section on joinder for a discussion of the significance of those classifications of a counterclaim.

★   (4) Cross-Claim

A cross-claim is a claim by one party against a co-party (e.g., Defendant 1 v. Defendant 2), which arises from the same transaction or occurrence that is the subject matter of the original action or of a counterclaim. Fed. R. Civ. P. 13(g). For example, Defendant 1's answer could assert, as a cross-claim against Defendant 2, a claim arising out of the same transaction or occurrence of any claim between Plaintiff and Defendants 1 and 2.

c) Answer to Counterclaim

A party defending against a counterclaim may file an answer to the counterclaim.

d) Answer to Crossclaim

A party defending against a crossclaim may file an answer to the counterclaim.

e) Reply to an Answer

A party may file a reply to an answer only if the court orders it.

★★★   4)   <u>TRANSACTION OR OCCURRENCE</u>

Federal courts consider several factors when determining whether different claims arise out of the same transaction or occurrence. Generally, they consider these factors when making that determination for either cross-claims or compulsory counterclaims. 6 Charles Alan Wright et al., *Federal Practice and Procedure Civil* §§ 1410, 1431 at 277 (2010). This outline further addresses compulsory counterclaims later. The factors include:

- same issues: whether the issues of law and fact in the claim and the cross-claim (or compulsory counterclaim) are nearly identical;
- same evidence: whether the identical evidence would refute or support the claim and the cross-claim (or compulsory counterclaim);
- logical relationship: whether a logical relationship exists between the claim and the cross-claim (or compulsory counterclaim), and
- *res judicata*: whether *res judicata* would preclude a later lawsuit on the cross-claim (or compulsory counterclaim).

Id., e.g., *Q Int'l Courier, Inc. v. Smoak*, 441 F.3d 214, 219 (4th Cir. 2006) (compulsory counterclaim).

a) Factor(s) May Support "Transaction or Occurrence"

The existence of any of those factors sustains a conclusion that the "transaction or occurrence" requirement is satisfied. 6 Wright et al., § 1410 at 58; e.g., *Glass v. IDS Fin. Serv., Inc.*, 778 F. Supp. 1029, 1061–62 (D. Minn. 1991). The third factor, which concerns a logical relationship, is the most often considered one. 6 Wright et al., § 1410 at 61.

b) Supplemental Jurisdiction

Cross-claims that fulfill the foregoing requirements for a "transaction or occurrence" presumptively fulfill the requirements of a "common nucleus of operative fact" and are subject to a federal court's supplemental jurisdiction. 13 Wright et al., § 3523, at 165–73. This outline addresses supplemental jurisdiction in an earlier section.

★★ 5) AMENDMENT OF PLEADINGS

A party may amend a pleading <u>once</u> as a matter of right within 21 days after serving it. If the pleading is one to which a responsive pleading is required, the party may amend it the earlier of either:

- 21 days after service of a responsive pleading; or
- 21 days after service of a Rule 12(b), (e), or (f) motion.

Otherwise, a party may amend the party's pleading only by leave of court or by written consent of the adverse party; and leave must be freely given when justice so requires. Fed. R. Civ. P. 15(a). The Supreme Court has held that amendments should be permitted unless such amendment results in a form of injustice.

Categories of injustice include:

- undue delay;
- bad faith or dilatory motive;
- repeated failure to cure defects by amendment;
- undue prejudice to the party opposing the amendment; or
- futility of the amendment.

A party must plead in response to an amended pleading within the time remaining for response to the original pleading or within 14 days after service of the amended pleading, whichever period may be longer, unless the court otherwise orders. Further amendments are permitted at a court's discretion. Leave to amend is liberally granted.

★   a)   Relation Back Doctrine

              (1)   New Claim

When the claim or defense asserted in an amended pleading arises out of the conduct, transaction, or occurrence set forth or attempted to be set forth in the original pleading, the amendment will be treated as if it was filed on the date of the original pleading.

              (2)   New Party

A common bar exam issue involves the addition of a new party after the statute of limitations has expired. For example, suppose a plaintiff sues a defendant shortly before the statute of limitations expires. After the statute of limitation expires, the plaintiff amends the complaint to add a different defendant. The action against the new defendant will satisfy the statute of limitations only if *both* the notice and mistake requirements are satisfied.

                     (a)   Notice

Under the notice requirement, an amended pleading adding a new party will relate back to the original pleading with regards to the statute of limitations if the new party had notice of the suit, such that it would not be prejudiced in being required to respond.

                     (b)   Mistake

Under the mistake requirement, an amended pleading adding a new party will relate back to the original pleading with regards to the statute of limitations if the new party knew or should have known that, but for a mistake in the identification of the proper party, it would have been served earlier.

      6)   <u>SUPPLEMENTAL PLEADINGS</u>

A supplemental pleading is used to set forth events that have happened since the filing date of a prior pleading that is sought to be supplemented. Leave of court, after giving notice to all other parties and making a motion to file a supplemental pleading, must be obtained to serve such a supplemental pleading. The courts' practice is usually liberal in allowing the filing of a supplemental pleading.

★★   C.   Rule 11

1)   SIGNATURE REQUIREMENT

Every pleading, motion, or other paper of a party represented by an attorney must be signed by at least one attorney of record. If an attorney willfully violates Rule 11, the attorney may be subjected to disciplinary action.

2)   REPRESENTATIONS

By presenting a filing to the court, a party or attorney makes several representations.

a)   No Improper Purpose

By presenting a filing to the court, an attorney or party represents that the claim, defense, request, demand, objection, contention, or argument is not presented or maintained for any improper purpose, such as to harass or to cause unnecessary delay or needless increase in the cost of litigation.

b)   Legal Grounding

By presenting a filing to the court, an attorney or party represents that the claims, defenses, and other legal contentions therein are warranted by existing law or by a non-frivolous argument for the extension, modification, or reversal of existing law or the establishment of new law.

c)   Evidentiary Support

By presenting a filing to the court, an attorney or party represents that the allegations and other factual contentions have evidentiary support or, if specifically so identified, are likely to have evidentiary support after a reasonable opportunity for further investigation or discovery.

d)   Denials

By presenting a filing to the court, an attorney or party represents that the denials of factual contentions are warranted on the evidence or, if specifically so identified, are reasonably based on a lack of information or belief.

3)   PROCESS FOR SANCTIONS

If, after notice and a reasonable opportunity to respond, a court finds that Rule 11 has been violated, the court may impose an appropriate sanction upon the lawyers, law firms, or parties that have committed, or are responsible for the violation.

Sanctions may be imposed either by motion or on the court's own initiative.

a)   By Motion

A motion for sanctions must describe the specific conduct alleged to have violated Rule 11. The motion should not be filed with the court unless, within 21 days after service of the motion, the challenged filing is not withdrawn or appropriately corrected. If warranted, the court may award to the party prevailing on the motion the reasonable expenses and attorney's fees incurred in presenting or opposing the motion.

For example, a party may serve a motion for sanctions on an opposing party alleging that the opposing party violated Rule 11 by bringing a frivolous claim. If the opposing party does not correct the complained of action within 21 days, the party requesting sanctions may file the motion for sanctions with the court.

b)   On Court's Initiative

On its own initiative, a court may enter an order describing the specific conduct that appears to violate Rule 11 and direct a lawyer, law firm, or party to withdraw or correct the questioned filing, or to show cause why it has not violated the Rule.

4)   NATURE OF SANCTIONS

A sanction imposed for violation of Rule 11 is limited to that which is sufficient to deter repetition of the conduct or comparable conduct by others similarly situated. The sanction may include:

- non-monetary directives,
- an order to pay a penalty into court, or,
- if imposed on motion and warranted for effective deterrence, an order directing payment to the movant of some or all of the reasonable attorney's fees and other expenses incurred as a direct result of the violation.

★   D.   Joinder of Parties and Claims

Joinder refers to the addition of claims or parties to a case that are beyond the scope of the initial pleadings such as a complaint and an answer.

★
1)   JOINDER OF CLAIMS

The requirements of subject-matter jurisdiction and personal jurisdiction must be satisfied with respect to each claim that is joined in an existing federal case.

a)   Compulsory Joinder of Claims

(1)   *Res Judicata*

Due to the claim preclusion doctrine of *res judicata*, a party should present a complete claim to the court. Although a party is not required to present the entire claim, if the party fails to do so, the party will be barred from bringing any other related claim in a later suit. A court conducts a transaction test to determine whether two separate requests for relief arise from the same claim for *res judicata* purposes.

(2)   Compulsory Counterclaims from Same Transaction

A defending party must put forward any claim that the defending party possesses:

> against an opposing party if the claim . . . arises out of the transaction or occurrence that is the subject matter of the opposing party's claim.

The failure to assert such a counterclaim precludes its assertion in a subsequent action. Fed. R. Civ. P. 13(a)(1)(A).

b)   Permissive Joinder of Claims

(1)   Great Discretion

A party enjoys great discretion regarding which claims may be joined in the parties' pleadings. The Rules allow for liberal joinder of different and alternative claims in a cause of action provided that the requirements of subject-matter jurisdiction and personal jurisdiction are satisfied with respect to each claim.

(2)   Permissive Counterclaims of Any Claims

A defending party may assert any counterclaim that the defending party possesses. The failure to assert a permissive counterclaim does not preclude its assertion in a subsequent action.

(3)   Cross-Claims

A defendant may assert a claim regarding the same transaction against a third party that is already involved in the litigation (i.e., co-defendant).

★   2)   JOINDER OF PARTIES

The Rules address the addition of a person as a party to a counterclaim or cross-claim.

a)   Compulsory Joinder of Parties

The Rules govern which persons must be joined in an action, and provide that these two types of parties are subject to compulsory joinder:

- necessary parties; and
- indispensable parties.

(1) Necessary Parties

A party is a necessary party if, in the person's absence, complete relief cannot be accorded among those parties who are already litigating a case. A necessary party must be joined if feasible. Joinder may not be possible in certain circumstances. For example, joinder may destroy diversity of citizenship for the purposes of subject-matter jurisdiction. Under those circumstances, the court must determine if the party sought to be joined is indispensable.

(2) Indispensable Parties

An indispensable party is a party without which a case cannot proceed if that party cannot be joined. When determining whether a party is indispensable, a court will generally examine the following factors:

- the extent to which a judgment rendered without the party might prejudice an absentee or existing parties;
- whether the prejudice can be lessened or avoided by appropriately shaping the relief granted;
- whether adequate relief can be granted without the absentee; and
- whether the plaintiff has an adequate remedy if the action is dismissed for non-joinder.

Several decided cases have held that causes of action seeking the rescission of a contract must be dismissed unless all parties to the contract, and any others having a substantial interest in it, can be joined. Moreover, when ownership of real property is involved in litigation, any and all people who possess an interest in that property are almost always considered indispensable parties.

b) Permissive Joinder

(1) Permissive Joinder of Plaintiffs

Multiple plaintiffs may join claims against a defendant in a single action when those claims arise out of a single event and share at least one common issue of law or fact. Rule 20(a)(1) states that:

> Persons may join in one action as plaintiffs if: (A) they assert any right to relief jointly, severally, or in the alternative with respect to or arising out of the same transaction, occurrence, or series of transactions or occurrences; and (B) any question of law or fact common to all plaintiffs will arise in the action.

(2) Permissive Joinder of Defendants

Just as a multiple plaintiffs may join in an action, a plaintiff may join multiple defendants in an action when the claims against each defendant arise from a single transaction and share a common issue of fact or law. The permissive joinder rule allows a plaintiff to choose and name the defendants but does not require that a plaintiff name all defendants who might be joined. Rule 20(a)(2) provides that:

> Persons -- as well as a vessel, cargo, or other property subject to admiralty process in rem -- may be joined in one action as defendants if: (A) any right to relief is asserted against them jointly, severally, or in the alternative with respect to or arising out of the same transaction, occurrence, or series of transactions or occurrences; and (B) any question of law or fact common to all defendants will arise in the action.

★★   c)   Independent Basis for Subject-Matter Jurisdiction Required

The Rules do not independently confer subject-matter jurisdiction in cases of joinder. The Rules simply provide the mechanism for joining claims over which that court may exercise subject-matter jurisdiction. Thus, joinder may be defeated when the court lacks subject-matter jurisdiction over a joined claim.

3)   MISCELLANEOUS JOINDER CONCEPTS

★   a)   Intervention

Intervention is a procedure that permits a non-party to participate in ongoing litigation in order to protect an interest that may be affected.

(1)   Intervention of Right

A non-party has a right to intervene in an action when a federal statute confers an unconditional right upon the non-party applicant to intervene in ongoing litigation. For example, the United States can always intervene in any action challenging the constitutionality of a federal statute. Moreover, intervention is of right when, under certain circumstances, the applicant asserts an interest which relates to the property or transaction that is the subject of the litigation.

(2)   Permissive Intervention

Intervention is permitted when a court determines that the interests of the original parties would not be prejudiced by allowing a nonparty applicant to participate in the ongoing litigation. A non-party applicant is entitled to intervene when its position is similar to that of a necessary party. If the applicant would be substantially affected by a determination that is made in the litigation, the applicant would usually be entitled to intervene.

★★   b)   Third-Party Practice

A defending party may bring a third-party complaint against a third party. The defending party becomes a third-party plaintiff and the non-party becomes a third-party defendant.

(1)   Impleader

The process of bringing a third-party complaint is called impleader. Impleader is appropriate only when a defending party, as a third-party plaintiff, makes a claim for some kind of derivative or secondary liability against a third-party defendant. In other words, the third-party plaintiff must assert that the third-party defendant is responsible for all or part of damages stemming from the claim against the third-party plaintiff. A third-party complaint would be appropriate when alleging liability due to indemnity, suretyship, subrogation, or contribution and warranty from parties other than joint tortfeasors.

For example, suppose a truck belonging to a trucking company hits a car at an intersection, resulting in injury to the car and driver. If the car's driver sues the trucking company, the trucking company may bring a third-party complaint against the truck driver based on a claim for indemnity.

(2)   When Motion Required

A potential third-party plaintiff does not need leave of court to serve a third-party complaint if no more than 14 days have passed since the party served its original answer. If more than 14 days have passed since filing its answer, then the third-party plaintiff must file a motion for leave to file the third-party complaint. The motion should state the defending party's reasons for joining the non-party in a case.

(3)   Any Defending Party May Serve Third-Party Complaint

Any party against whom a claim is asserted may serve a third-party complaint. For example, the following parties may serve a third-party complaint against a non-party:

- original plaintiff against whom a claim is made;
- original defendant;
- third-party defendant;
- any other party against whom a claim is made.

(4)   Separating or Striking Claim

After a third-party complaint is served, a court has discretion to strike the claim if it is unmeritorious. Alternatively, the court may sever the third-party claim or order a separate trial.

(5)   Qualifies under Supplemental Jurisdiction

A third-party claim falls within a federal court's supplement jurisdiction. Therefore, no independent ground for subject matter jurisdiction is required.

★ c) Interpleader

Interpleader permits a party (as a "stakeholder") to avoid the risk of potential multiple liability by requiring two or more other claimants with actual or potential claims against the stakeholder to assert their respective claims in one suit. Interpleader can be brought either as a separate action, a cross-claim, or a counterclaim. Interpleader is a somewhat infrequently used, but significant, joinder device whose core function is to save stakeholders, such as bailees and insurance companies, from logically inconsistent liability to claimants with respect to a single thing or asset.

Interpleader stems from a basic proposition of justice that the law should not require a stakeholder to give the same thing to two or more different claimants. For example, if a first bailee checks a coat at a cloakroom and a second bailee comes along claiming to be the owner of the coat and that the first bailee stole the coat from the second bailee, the bailor should have a way to avoid the threat of two independent actions with the possibility of orders in each to give the same coat to a different bailee. Similarly and more realistically, a life insurance company ought to have some way to protect itself against inconsistent claims to a single benefit. That might occur if an insured designates a first spouse as a beneficiary but has purportedly become remarried to a second spouse. In that instance the first spouse might challenge the validity of the divorce proceeding, and consequently claim an entitlement to the proceeds of the policy in contravention of the second spouse's claim.

d) Consolidation

When actions involving a common question of law or fact are pending before a court, the court may order a joint hearing or trial of any or all of the matters that are in issue in those actions. Fed. R. Civ. P. 42(a). The court may order that all of those actions be consolidated into one case. The court may make any orders concerning proceedings in that case which would tend to avoid unnecessary costs or delay. The interests sought to be promoted through consolidation of the actions are judicial expediency and efficiency.

e) Severance

A court, in furtherance of convenience or to avoid prejudice, may order a separate trial of any claim, cross-claim, counterclaim, or third-party claim. Fed. R. Civ. P. 42(b). The court may also order a separate trial of any separate issue or of any number of claims, cross-claims, counterclaims, third-party claims, or issues. The court must always preserve the right of trial by jury.

★ 4) CLASS ACTIONS

a) Certification Prerequisites

In order to bring an action as a class action, plaintiffs must satisfy several certification requirements.

(1)   Numerosity

In order to bring an action as a class action, plaintiffs must demonstrate that the numerous members of a class render joinder of them all impractical.

(2)   Commonality

In order to bring an action as a class action, plaintiffs must demonstrate that common questions of law and fact exist among the members of the class.

(3)   Typicality

In order to bring an action as a class action, plaintiffs must demonstrate that the claims of the representatives and the members of the class are typical. The claims will be considered typical if all they arise from a single event or if they all are based on common legal theories. *Rall v. Medtronic,* 1986 WL 22271 (D. Nev. 1986).

(4)   Adequacy of Representation

In order to bring an action as a class action, plaintiffs must satisfy the adequacy of representation requirement. The requirement involves a two-part inquiry. First, a court must ask whether the representative's interests are aligned closely enough with the other class members to ensure fair representation of the absentee class members. Second, the court must ensure that the counsel for the class are experienced and qualified to carry out the litigation in order to fairly and adequately protect the interests of the class.

b)   Maintenance

A lawsuit meeting the certification prerequisites may be maintained as a class action if either there is a risk of inconsistency or class questions predominate.

(1)   Risk of Inconsistency

A lawsuit meeting the certification prerequisites may be maintained as a class action if the prosecution of separate actions by or against the members of the class would create a risk of inconsistency or varying adjudications.

(2)   Class Questions Predominate

A lawsuit meeting the certification prerequisites may be maintained as a class action if questions of law or fact common to the members of the class predominate over any questions that only affect individual members. Under these circumstances, a class action is superior to all other available methods for the fair and efficient adjudication of the controversy.

c)   Adequate Notice Must Be Given to the Class

In order to maintain a class action, adequate notice of the lawsuit must be given to the class. Sometimes, the provision of actual notice to every class member may be impossible. In that event, a court, in its discretion, may order the provision of such notice that it deems necessary to protect the interests of the class and the parties.

★★★   E.   **Discovery, Disclosure, and Sanctions**

Discovery is the process of gathering information (potential evidence) in preparation for a trial. A party may serve discovery requests on other parties and non-parties.

1)   <u>DISCOVERY METHODS AND CONCEPTS</u>

A party may utilize many discovery methods to gather evidence.

a)   Depositions

A deposition is a legal proceeding in which a party or attorney questions a witness under oath. The testifying witness is called the deponent. A deposition usually occurs before a trial and takes place outside of court.

(1)   Oral Examination

A party desiring to take an oral deposition must give <u>reasonable notice</u> to every other party, stating the time, place, names, and addresses of all persons to deposed. Fed. R. Civ. P. 30.

(2)   Written Questions

A party may take a deposition upon written questions. Fed. R. Civ. P. 31.

★   (3)   Corporate Deposition

A party may depose a corporation or other organization. Fed. R. Civ. P. 30(b). The party must notify the corporation or organization, and designate matters on which examination is requested. *Id.* The organization must designate a person or people to testify as to matters known or reasonably available to the organization.

(4)   Subpoena

A subpoena is a legal document ordering someone to appear somewhere. A party may serve a subpoena on the person to be examined by deposition directing the person to appear for questioning at a certain place at a specified date and time.

★   (a)   Subpoena *Duces Tecum*

A subpoena *duces tecum* is a subpoena that includes a request that the person produce certain documents. A party may serve a subpoena *duces tecum* on someone requiring the production of documents relevant to a dispute. The party that issues the subpoena may review the materials in advance of the deposition, and question the witness about them during the deposition.

★   (5)   Deposition Before Action Is Filed

A petitioner may attempt to have a deposition before an actual case is filed in court. Fed. R. Civ. P. 27(a). A person or entity seeking to have a pre-filing deposition may file a verified petition in the federal district court in the county of the residence of any expected adverse party.

★   (6)   Use of Depositions at Trial

So far as otherwise admissible under the Federal Rules of Evidence, all or any portion of a deposition (if necessary to be fair), may be submitted at a trial:

- to impeach a deponent as a witness;
- for any purpose if the deponent was a corporate representative and the evidence is used against the corporation; or
- for any purpose if the deponent is dead or unavailable because he or she is outside of a court's subpoena power.

Fed. R. Civ. P. 32.

(7)   Disclosed Expert

A disclosed expert may be deposed, but only after disclosure of the expert's report (if required under the Rules).

b)   Interrogatories

★★ Interrogatories are written questions asked by one party of an opposing party, who must answer them in writing under oath. Interrogatories may only be served on a party. Fed. R. Civ. P. 33. The answers to interrogatories can be used as evidence in the trial.

(1)   When Opposing Party May Substitute Access for Answer

The opposing party may substitute access to documents or electronically stored information for an interrogatory answer if the burden of obtaining the answer will be substantially the same for either party.

★   (2)   Limitations Apply as to Questions and Answers

Absent court permission to ask more questions, a set of interrogatories are limited to 25 total questions, *including subparts*. Fed. R. Civ. P. 33(a).

★   (3)   Time to Respond

A party must serve answers to interrogatories within 30 days of being served. Fed. R. Civ. P. 33(b)(3).

★   c)   Requests for Admission

A request for admission is a written statement served by one party, on another party, requesting that the responding party admit or deny the truth of a statement. Fed. R. Civ. P. 36. A party may serve a request for admission on any other party regarding any issue of fact. A party cannot request an admission regarding an issue of law.

(1)   Time to Respond

A party must serve a response to a request for admission within 30 days of being served. A failure to respond may be construed as an admission.

★   d)   Request for Production

A party may request any other party to produce and/or permit inspection or copying of designated documents, electronically stored information, or other tangible things. Fed. R. Civ. P. 34(a).

(1)   Types of Electronically Stored Information

Types of electronically stored information include writings, graphs, drawings, charts, sound recordings, photographs, images, and other data or data compilations. The electronically stored information may be stored in any medium from which it can be procured either directly or, if necessary, after the responding party translates it into a reasonably usable form. The request may specify the form(s) for producing the electronically stored information.

(2)   Time to Respond

A party must serve a response to a request for production within 30 days of being served. The response must either permit inspection of the items, or object to the request for some specified reason (e.g., work-product protection). The response may object to the requested form for producing the electronically stored information (the "Form"). If the responding party objects to the requested Form, or if the request does not specify a Form, then the responding party must state the Form that it intends to use.

(3)   Production of Documents or
            Electronically Stored Information

Unless the parties agree or the court orders otherwise, the following procedures apply:

- a party need not produce the same electronically stored information in more than one form;

- if a request does not specify a Form, then a party must produce the electronically stored information in the form that is ordinarily maintained or in a reasonably usable form; and
- a party must produce documents as they are maintained in the usual course of business or must label and organize the documents to fit the request's categories.

(4)   Production of Documents from Non-party by Subpoena

A party may also seek the production of discoverable documents from a non-party by the use of a subpoena *duces tecum* (discussed above).

e)   Physical or Mental Examination

A party may request an examination of the mental or physical condition of a party by a physician, only upon a motion and good cause shown. Fed. R. Civ. P. 35(a). The physical or mental condition of the party must be an issue in controversy. The party requesting the examination must furnish the examined party with all earlier examinations to which the party may have access, including test results. Fed. R. Civ. P. 35(b). The examined party must then make a similar disclosure in return.

f)   Expert Testimony

When knowledge of a technical subject matter might be helpful to a trier of fact (e.g., judge or jury), a person having special training or experience in that technical field is permitted to state the person's opinion concerning those technical matters, even though the person was not present at an event that relates to a disputed issue. For example, an arson expert could testify about the probable cause of a suspicious fire. The information that an expert relies on to testify, or to prepare a report that the expert relies upon when testifying, is discoverable.

★   2)   REQUIRED DISCLOSURES

In a federal action, the parties are required to produce certain evidence without a discovery request.

a)   Initial Disclosures

The parties in a federal case must make initial disclosures to an opponent early during the case. Fed. R. Civ. P. 26(a)(1). A party must provide the initial disclosures to each opposing party's counsel. Initial disclosures include:

- names and contact information of all persons likely to have discoverable information;
- a copy or description of relevant "documents, electronically stored information, and tangible things" within the parties' possession;
- a computation of each category of damages that are sought and the documents upon which the computations are based, such as documents showing injury; and

- any insurance agreement under which an insurance company might be liable to satisfy a judgment.

Initial disclosures must be made based on the information reasonably available to the party. The party cannot fail to make initial disclosures simply because it has not fully investigated, or because another party has not made disclosures or has not made adequate disclosures.

(1)   Proceedings Exempt from Initial Disclosure Requirement

Some proceedings are exempt from the initial disclosure requirement. Exempt proceedings include:

- an action for review on an administrative record;
- a forfeiture action arising from a federal statute;
- a proceeding to challenge a criminal conviction or sentence;
- an action brought by incarcerated *pro se* (i.e., self-representing) litigants;
- an action to enforce or quash an administrative summons or subpoena;
- an action by the United States to recover benefit payments;
- an action by the United States to collect on a student loan;
- a proceeding ancillary to a proceeding in another court; and
- an action to enforce an arbitration award.

(2)   Time for Initial Disclosures

A party must make initial disclosures within 14 days after the required conference of the parties addressed below, unless another time is set by stipulation or court order, or a party objects at the conference. For parties who are joined after the required conference, initial disclosures must be made within 30 days after being served or joined.

b)   Disclosure of Expert Testimony

A party must disclose the identity of any expert who may be used at trial. Fed. R. Civ. P. 26(a)(2)(A). Unless otherwise directed by the court, a party must make the disclosure at least 90 days before the date trial is set to begin. If the expert testimony will be used solely to rebut evidence indentified by another party, then the disclosure must be made 30 days after the other party's disclosure.

(1)   Expert Required to Provide Written Report

If an expert is required to provide a written report as part of the expert's engagement, then the disclosure of the expert's identity must also include the report. Fed. R. Civ. P. 26(a)(2)(B). The report must contain the following information:

- all opinions that will be expressed and the reasons for those opinions;
- facts or data considered in forming opinions;
- exhibits that will be used to summarize or support opinions;

- qualifications, including publications within past 10 years;
- list of all other cases in past 4 years where witness has testified as expert; and
- compensation that will be paid for expert testimony.

(2)   Expert Not Required to Provide Written Report

If an expert is not required to provide a written report as part of the expert's engagement, then the disclosure of the expert's identity must indicate the subject matter of the expert's testimony and a summary of the expert's opinions and facts. Fed. R. Civ. P. 26(a)(2)(C).

c)   Pretrial Disclosures

In addition to initial and expert witness disclosures, a party must provide the following information that may be presented at trial for purposes other than the impeachment of a witness:

- the identity of and contact information for each witness who may be called to testify;
- a designation of those witnesses whose testimony is to be presented by deposition, along with a transcript of relevant portions of each deposition; and
- an identification of each document or exhibit that may be offered as evidence at the trial.

(1)   Must Make Pretrial Disclosures 30 Days before Trial

Pretrial disclosures must be made 30 days before trial.

(2)   Party May File Objections within 14 Days after Disclosure

A party may file objections to such information within 14 days after disclosure by the other party.

3)   DISCOVERY SCOPE AND LIMITS

★   a)   Broad Scope of Discovery

The scope of discovery is broad and construed liberally. A party is entitled to discovery regarding any information that is relevant to any party's claim or defense, provided that the information is neither privileged nor attorney work-product. Fed. R. Civ. P. 26(b)(1). However, a court can order discovery of any relevant matter, even privileged information, upon a showing of good cause. Relevant information does not have to be admissible at trial, so long as the information might lead to discovery of admissible evidence. The relevance of information sought by a party during discovery will be determined on a case-by-case basis, depending on the circumstances and the facts. *Hill v. Motel 6*, 205 F.R.D. 490 (S.D. Ohio 2001).

b)   Limitations on Frequency and Extent

A court *may* limit the scope of discovery, including the number or length of depositions and interrogatories, as well as the number of requests for production.

A trial court *must* limit the extent or frequency of discovery if:

- the discovery is unreasonably duplicative or cumulative, or the party can obtain it from another source that is more convenient, less expensive, or less burdensome;
- the party requesting discovery has sufficient opportunity to obtain the information by discovery; or
- the expense or burden of the proposed discovery outweighs its likely benefit.

Fed. R. Civ. P. 26(b)(2)(C).

(1)   Specific Limitations on Electronically Stored Information

A party does not have to provide discovery of electronically stored information from sources that the party designates as not reasonably accessible because of cost or *undue burden*. On motion for a protective order or to compel discovery, the party from whom discovery is requested must prove that the electronically stored information is not reasonably accessible because of cost or undue burden. If the party proves that, then the trial court may still order discovery from those designated sources if the requesting party shows good cause. The trial court may state conditions for the discovery. Fed. R. Civ. P. 26(b)(2)(B).

★★   c)   Attorney Work-Product and Related Concepts

A party may not obtain discovery evidence that qualifies as attorney work-product. Attorney work-product may be both intangible, such as a discussion, and tangible, such as a document. *Hickman v. Taylor*, 329 U.S. 495 (1947) (recognizing qualified work-product immunity); Fed. R. Civ. P. 26(b)(3).

★   (1)   Materials Prepared in Anticipation of Litigation or for Trial

Generally, materials that are prepared in *anticipation of litigation* or for trial (by or for a party or its representative), are protected from discovery. Fed. R. Civ. P. 26(b)(3)(A). A party's representative can include its lawyer, consultant, indemnitor, surety, insurer, or agent. *Id.*

For example, investigative reports or accident reports, which a party routinely completes after an accident, are protected from discovery *only if* they are prepared to address a threat of imminent litigation. *Broadnax v. ABF Freight Sys., Inc.*, 180 F.R.D. 343, 346 (N.D. Ill. 1998); *Wikel v. Wal-Mart Stores, Inc.*, 197 F.R.D. 493 (N.D. Okla. 2000). In the absence of any threat of litigation when the reports are completed, they are discoverable. *Id.*; Fed. R. Civ. P. 26(b)(3) (Advisory Committee's Note).

Any person may obtain their own previous statements about the action or its subject matter simply upon request. If the request is refused, the person may request a court order and be awarded expenses.

(a)   Substantial Need and Undue Hardship Exception

Another party may discover these protected materials if:

- the materials are otherwise discoverable;
- the party shows its substantial need for the materials to prepare its case; and
- the party is unable, without undue hardship, to obtain the substantial equivalent of the materials by other means. *Id.*

(i)   Required Protection

If a court orders discovery of materials prepared in anticipation of litigation or for trial, then the court must protect against disclosure of the *mental impressions*, opinions, conclusions, or legal theories of a party's lawyer or representative about the litigation. Fed. R. Civ. P. 26(b)(3)(B).

(2)   Expert Witness Retained in Preparation for Trial

The attorney work-product protection also provides "trial-preparation protection" to several types of trial preparation regarding expert witnesses. Fed. R. Civ. P. 26(b)(4)(B)-(C).

(a)   Draft Reports or Disclosures

Drafts of any reports or disclosures made by expert witnesses are protected from disclosure "regardless of the form in which the draft is recorded." Fed. R. Civ. P. 26(b)(4)(B).

(b)   Communications between Lawyer and Expert

Communications between a party's lawyer and expert witness, "regardless of the form of the communications," are protected from disclosure, unless the communications:

- concern compensation for the expert's testimony or study;
- identify data or facts that the lawyer provided and that the expert considered in forming their opinions; or
- identify assumptions that the lawyer provided and that the expert relied on.

Fed. R. Civ. P. 26(b)(4)(C).

Note that these communications can take any form, such as discussions, as they are not limited to only materials such as tangible things and documents. *Id.*

(i)   Experts Employed only for Trial Preparation

Generally, a party may not discover facts known or opinions held by an expert who is employed by a party's lawyer solely for trial preparation, and who is not expected to be called as a witness at trial. However, this information may be discoverable upon a showing of exceptional circumstances if it is impracticable for the party to obtain facts or opinions on the same subject, by any other means.

(c)   Payment for Expert Disclosure

The party seeking discovery must pay the expert a reasonable fee for the time spent responding to discovery. If a non-testifying expert is required to disclose facts or opinions, the party seeking such discovery must also pay the other party a fair portion of the fees and expenses incurred in obtaining the expert's facts and opinions.

(3)   Claiming Attorney Work-Product Protection

To withhold otherwise discoverable information based on a claim of privilege or a claim that the information is protected as trial preparation material:

- The party must expressly make the claim;
- The party must describe the nature of the documents, communications, or tangible things not disclosed; and
- The party must make such description in a way that does not reveal the privileged information but allows the other party to assess the claim.

If information subject to a claim of privilege or of trial preparation material has already been produced in discovery, then the party may notify any party that received the information, of the claim. After such notification, the receiving party must promptly return, sequester, or destroy the information. A party must take reasonable steps to retrieve the information if it has already been disclosed, and may promptly present the information to the court for a ruling on the claim.

4)   <u>PROTECTIVE ORDERS</u>

In the discovery context, a protective order is an order protecting a party from producing discovery. A party or person from whom discovery is being sought may file a motion for a protective order. Fed. R. Civ. P. 26(c). The motion must certify that the requesting party has in good faith conferred or attempted to confer with the other parties to try to resolve the dispute. The court may make any order that justice requires in order to protect a party or person from annoyance, embarrassment, oppression, undue burden, or expense.

A protective order may do any of the following:

- forbid disclosure or discovery;
- specify the terms for the disclosure or discovery, including time and place;
- set a discovery method;
- forbid inquiry into certain matters or limit the scope of disclosure or discovery of certain matters;
- designate the persons who may be present while discovery is conducted;
- require that discovery be sealed;

- require that trade secrets or confidential information not be revealed, or revealed only in specified ways;
- require that parties file documents or information in sealed envelopes, only to be opened by court order.

a) Court Must Weigh Interests

When deciding whether to allow discovery resisted by a party, a trial judge must weigh an alleged privacy interest that disclosure would infringe upon against the interest of the party requesting discovery. *Eckstein Marine Serv., Inc. v. M/V Basin Pride,* 168 F.R.D. 38 (W.D. La. 1996). The trial judge can review materials *in camera* (i.e., in chambers) to identify and redact (e.g., block out) irrelevant, sensitive, or private matters prior to permitting discovery of any other part of these materials. *Id.*

b) Compelling Discovery

A motion to compel discovery is a motion requesting that a trial court require a person to make disclosures, respond to a discovery request, or make more detailed disclosures/responses to a discovery request. Fed. R. Civ. P. 37(a)(2). A party may file a motion to compel a party to produce discovery if the party refuses to adequately respond to a discovery request. A party may also request that the court impose sanctions on a person that fails to comply with the court's order to compel discovery or otherwise obstructs discovery.

★   5)   SUPPLEMENTING DISCLOSURES

A party is under a duty to timely supplement or correct its discovery disclosures when the party learns that the disclosure or response is incomplete or incorrect in some material respect, and the additional or corrective information has not already been made known to the party during discovery. Fed. R. Civ. P. 26(e). A party is also under a duty to amend its answers to interrogatories, requests for production, and admissions, if new information comes to light that impacts its previous disclosures that are contained in those types of discovery responses. However, this rule does not apply to depositions. Nonetheless, if a party's expert witness must disclose a report, then the party has a duty to supplement both information contained in the report and information provided during a deposition of the expert. Fed. R. Civ. P. 26(e)(2).

★   6)   REQUIRED INITIAL CONFERENCE OF THE PARTIES

In federal court actions, unless otherwise directed by the court, the parties must hold an initial conference to plan the discovery process as soon as practicable, or at least 21 days before a scheduling conference. At the initial conference, the parties must:

- consider claims and defenses, and the possibilities for settling or resolving the case;
- make or arrange for initial disclosures;
- discuss any issues regarding preserving discoverable information; and
- develop a discovery plan.

a)   Discovery Plan

Within 14 days after the initial conference, the parties must submit a written report to the court outlining the discovery plan. The discovery plan must:

- state the parties' proposals on when initial disclosures were or will be made, or what changes should be made to the timing, form, or requirements for initial disclosures;
- the subjects on which discovery will be needed;
- when discovery should be completed and the scope of discovery;
- any issues regarding discovery or electronically stored information;
- any issues about claims of privilege or trial preparation protection materials;
- changes that should be made to the limitations on discovery imposed by the Rules; and
- any protective or scheduling orders the court should enter.

b)   Electronically Stored Information; Metadata

At the initial conference, parties should specifically address the discovery or disclosure of electronically stored information, including the form(s) in which they should produce it, and whether production of metadata will occur. Fed. R. Civ. P. 26(f)(3)(C), (Advisory Committee's Note — 2006 Amendment).

7)   TIMING AND ORDER OF DISCOVERY

A party cannot seek discovery from any source before the required initial conference of the parties, other than in proceedings exempted from initial disclosure, or when allowed by stipulation or court order. Discovery can be made in any sequence unless otherwise ordered by the court for a parties' or witnesses' convenience or where the interests of justice dictate. Also, discovery by one party does not require any other party to delay its discovery.

8)   SIGNING DISCLOSURES AND DISCOVERY REQUESTS

All initial and pretrial disclosures, and every request, response, or objection must be signed by at least one attorney of record, or by the party if unrepresented. The signature must also include the signer's address, e-mail address, and telephone number.

a)   Person's Signature Certifies as to Disclosure, Request, Response

By signing, the person certifies that:
- a disclosure is complete and correct; and
- a discovery request or response is consistent with the law, not requested for an improper purpose, and not unreasonably burdensome.

b)   Consequences of Not Signing Discovery Qualifying Document

If a discovery qualifying document is not signed, the other party has no duty to act on it. The court may strike it unless a signature is promptly provided.

c)   Court May Impose Sanction for Certification Violating Rules

If a certification violates the Rules, then the court must impose an appropriate sanction, including reasonable expenses and attorney's fees, on the signer, the party on whose behalf the signer was acting, or both.

★   ### 9)   SANCTIONS FOR DISCOVERY VIOLATIONS

A trial court plays an integral role as the supervisor of discovery. A court may sanction parties or attorneys for unreasonable conduct during the discovery process. Fed. R. Civ. P. 37. Also, a court may require the parties to meet for discovery conferences to expedite the discovery process.

a)   Failure to Provide Electronically Stored Information

Other than under exceptional circumstances, a trial court may not impose sanctions upon a party for not providing electronically stored information lost on account of the routine, good-faith operation of an electronically stored information system. Fed. R. Civ. P. 37(e).

10)   DEFERENCE TO TRIAL COURT IN DISCOVERY DECISIONS

A trial court is afforded significant discretion in making discovery decisions. Accordingly, an appellate court would only overturn a trial court decision regarding discovery if the court abused its discretion. Thus, such trial court's decisions are entitled to significant deference on appeal.

F.   Adjudication without a Trial

Adjudication is the rendering of a judgment in a case. A legal action involves the entire legal process of dispute resolution. A dispute will not necessarily go through every phase of civil procedure before resulting in adjudication. Rather, adjudication of a case can occur with or without the case going to trial. Adjudication without a trial may occur by several means including summary judgment, default judgment, involuntary or voluntary dismissal, settlement, and alternative dispute resolution.

1)   VOLUNTARY DISMISSAL OF CLAIM

An action may be dismissed without court order:

- by the plaintiff alone by filing a notice of dismissal at any time before the adverse party serves an answer or a motion for summary judgment (whichever comes first); or
- by stipulation of dismissal signed by all parties who have appeared in the action.

Otherwise, the part(ies) seeking dismissal must obtain a court order. Unless otherwise stated, the first such dismissal is without prejudice. The second dismissal of an action based on or including the same claim may act as a judgment on the merits.

2) SETTLEMENT AND CONSENT JUDGMENT

The parties to a case can agree to settle the case out of court. The parties may set forth and sign their settlement agreement in a consent judgment (a judgment by consent or stipulation), which the court signs, enters on the record, and may enforce as a judgment. Although settlement does not technically constitute adjudication, it can have the same effect when the parties enter into a consent judgment.

3) OFFER OF JUDGMENT AND NOTICE OF ACCEPTANCE

At least 14 days before the trial date, a defendant may serve upon a plaintiff, an offer of judgment against the defendant for a particular amount of money or property. If the plaintiff provides a written notice of acceptance within 14 days, then either party may file the offer and notice, and the court clerk will enter judgment. Fed. R. Civ. P. 68(a). If the plaintiff does not accept the offer, and does not obtain a judgment more favorable than the offer, then the plaintiff must pay the costs of the trial from when the defendant made the offer. Fed. R. Civ. P. 68(d).

4) FEDERAL ALTERNATIVE DISPUTE RESOLUTION ACT OF 1998

All federal district courts must require that litigants consider the use of alternative dispute resolution (ADR) processes in civil litigation. 28 U.S.C. § 652. A federal district court must provide for the confidentiality of ADR processes and prohibit disclosure of confidential ADR communications.

G.   Pre-Trial Conference and Order

1)   PRE-TRIAL CONFERENCE

★

a)   Objectives of Conference

A court may direct the parties or attorneys to appear before it for a pre-trial conference for several purposes including:

- expediting the disposition of the action,
- establishing early and continuing control so that the case will not be protracted because of lack of management,
- discouraging wasteful pre-trial activities,
- improving the quality of the trial through more thorough preparation, and
- facilitating the settlement of the case.

The judge possesses discretion in planning and conducting the conference. Appearance of counsel at a pre-trial conference ordered by a federal district court is mandatory, although the Rules do not compel the court to conduct such a conference in every case. *Identiseal Corp. v. Positive Identification Sys., Inc.,* 560 F.2d 298 (7th Cir. 1977).

b) Authority of Counsel at Pre-Trial Conference

At least one of the attorneys for each party participating in a pre-trial conference must possess the authority to enter into stipulations and to make admissions regarding all matters that the participants may reasonably anticipate to be discussed. Fed. R. Civ. P. 16(c). If appropriate, the federal district court may require that a party or its representatives be present or reasonably available by telephone in order to consider possible settlement of the dispute.

c) Final Pre-trial Conference

If the federal district court holds a final pre-trial conference, it must be held as close to the time of trial as reasonable under the circumstances. Fed. R. Civ. P. 16(d). The participants at any such conference must formulate a plan for trial, including a program for facilitating the admission of evidence. The conference must be attended by at least one of the attorneys who will conduct the trial for each of the parties, and by any unrepresented parties.

d) Pre-trial Orders

After any pre-trial conference, an order must be entered reciting the action taken. Fed. R. Civ. P. 16(e). This order controls the subsequent course of the action unless it is modified by a subsequent order. The order following a final pre-trial conference will be modified only to prevent manifest injustice.

e) Sanctions

(1) Grounds for Sanctions

A court may issue such orders that are just, and among other options, may impose sanctions if:

- a party or the party's attorney fails to obey a scheduling or pre-trial order;
- no appearance is made on behalf of a party at a scheduling or pre-trial conference;
- a party or party's attorney is substantially unprepared to participate in the conference; or
- a party or party's attorney fails to participate in good faith.

Fed. R. Civ. P. 16(f).

(2) Types of Sanctions

In lieu of, or in addition to any other sanction, a judge can require a party, attorney, or both, to pay the reasonable expenses incurred because of any noncompliance. Some other more severe sanctions include striking pleadings, entering a default judgment, or dismissing a lawsuit. The latter two sanctions generally are proper "only when [a litigant's] misconduct is serious, repeated, contumacious, extreme, or otherwise inexcusable." *Bachier-Ortiz v. Colon-Mendoza,* 331 F.3d 193 (1st Cir. 2003). Unless grounds exist to believe that lesser sanctions would not ensure obedience to the judge's order, such sanctions should be imposed prior to ordering more severe ones. *Berry v. CIGNA/RSI-CIGNA,* 975 F.2d 1188 (5th Cir. 1992). Of course, sanctions can be challenged and reversed on appeal if they constitute an abuse of the judge's discretion in terms of whether they are just under the facts and their severity. *Link v. Wabash R.R. Co.,* 370 U.S. 626 (1962).

2) SCHEDULING ORDERS

After receiving the parties' discovery reports, a federal district court must enter a scheduling order that limits the time to:

- join other parties and to amend the pleadings;
- file motions; and
- complete discovery.

Fed. R. Civ. P. 16(b).

The scheduling order may also include:

- modifications of deadlines for required discovery disclosures (see Discovery section);
- the dates for any pre-trial conferences and trial; and
- any other appropriate matter given the circumstances of the case.

The order should be issued as soon as practicable. A schedule may not be modified except upon a showing of good cause and by leave of the court.

IV. JURY TRIALS

★★   **A. Right to a Jury Trial**

1) GENERAL – ACTIONS AT LAW

A party possesses a right to a jury trial in all actions at law (for damages) for claims exceeding a claim amount of $20. U.S. Const. amend. VII; Fed. R. Civ. P. 38(a). Pursuant to the Rules, any legal claims should be tried before any equitable claims are tried.

Rule 38(a) states that:

> The right of trial by jury as declared by the Seventh Amendment to the Constitution -- or as provided by a federal statute -- is preserved to the parties inviolate.

2)   EQUITABLE CLAIMS

A party asserting solely equitable claims or remedies does not have a right to a jury trial, but a party may possess both legal and equitable claims in one action.

3)   WAIVER OF THE RIGHT TO A JURY TRIAL

A party must file a jury trial demand within 14 days of the filing of the last pleading that is directed to the issue for which the basis of right to jury trial exists. Fed. R. Civ. P. 38(b). Otherwise, the right to a trial by jury is waived.

B.   Selection and Composition of Juries

1)   JURY SELECTION

Jury selection refers to the process of choosing the members of a jury. Prospective jurors receive a summons to appear in court. The parties and court then conduct jury selection. The prospective jurors comprise the jury panel from which the jurors are selected.

a)   Considerations Regarding Prospective Jurors

Parties entitled to a jury trial have a right to a jury selected at random from a *fair cross section of the community*. 28 U.S.C. § 1861.

(1)   Grounds for Disqualification from Serving on Jury

A person can serve on a jury unless the person

- is not a United States citizen,
- is under 18 years of age,
- is illiterate,
- is not fluent in English,
- is mentally or physically infirm, or
- has a criminal record.

28 U.S.C. § 1865(b).

(2)   Prohibited Grounds for Exclusion of Citizen from Serving

A citizen may not be excluded from serving as a juror based on the citizen's color, race, national origin, sex, religion, or economic status. 28 U.S.C. § 1862.

b)   Jury Selection Process

(1)   Voir Dire

Voir dire means to "speak the truth," and refers to the initial questioning of the prospective jurors to determine their qualifications and suitability.

(a)   Mechanics of Questioning

The trial court may either question the prospective jurors or permit the parties or lawyers to question them. Fed. R. Civ. P. 47(a).

If the court questions the jurors, then:

- the court must permit the parties or their lawyer to ask supplemental questions; or
- the court must ask supplemental questions it considers proper. *Id.*

(b)   Challenge to Jury Panel

At *voir dire*, a lawyer may object to the composition of the jury panel as not fulfilling constitutional or statutory prerequisites. For example, an attorney may challenge the jury panel on the basis that it does not represent a *fair cross section of the community*. 28 U.S.C. § 1870.

★★   (c)   Challenge to Prospective Juror

Each party alternately strikes (or challenges) prospective jurors from the array until the number of jurors needed for the jury is reached. At *voir dire*, a lawyer may object to a prospective juror by making either a challenge for cause or a peremptory challenge. *Id.*

(i)   Challenge for Cause

A party may make an unlimited number of challenges for cause on grounds that a juror:

- does not fulfill the statutory qualifications for jury duty; or
- has a bias or relationship to a party or the case. *Id.*

For example, a party may challenge a prospective juror for cause if the prospective juror worked for a party or owns stock in a party.

If a potential juror states that he can fairly consider the evidence, a court may take the statement into consideration.

(ii)   Peremptory Challenge

A peremptory challenge is the right to challenge a potential juror without stating a reason. A party could use a peremptory challenge to remove a prospective juror that is believed to have some social or occupational opinion that is not favorable to the party.

(A)   Number of Challenges

Each party may make <u>three peremptory challenges</u>. *Id.*; Fed. R. Civ. P. 47(b). A court may allow additional peremptory challenges.

        (B)   Multiple Parties Treated as One

<u>Multiple defendants</u> or <u>plaintiffs</u> may be considered a <u>single party</u> for the purposes of making challenges.

★   2)   <u>JURY COMPOSITION</u>

        a)   Number of Jurors

A jury must consist of a minimum of 6 and a maximum of 12 jurors. Fed. R. Civ. P. 48(a). Each juror must participate in the verdict unless the court excuses a juror for good cause. *Id.* citing Fed. R. Civ. P. 47(c).

        (1)   Good Cause

Under the proper circumstances, the court may excuse a juror during the jury deliberations without causing a mistrial. Fed. R. Civ. P. 47(c) (Advisory Committee's Notes -- 1991 Amendment). Examples of good cause include family emergency, sickness, or juror misconduct. *Id.*

C.   Requests for and Objections to Jury Instructions

        1)   <u>GENERAL</u>

After the close of the evidence, any party may serve written requests that the court instruct the jury on issues of law. Fed. R. Civ. P. 51(a). The court must inform the counsel of its proposed action upon the requests before they present their arguments to the jury. The court may instruct the jury after counsel finishes making their arguments.

        2)   <u>OBJECTIONS – PRESERVATION OF ERROR IN JURY CHARGE</u>

No party may assign as error the court's giving or failure to give a written instruction to the jury unless:

- the party objects with particularity for providing, or failing to provide, the written instruction;
- before the jury retires to consider its verdict.

The court must afford objecting counsel an opportunity to object outside of the jury's presence.

Fed. R. Civ. P. 51(b)-(c).

        3)   <u>JUDGE CANNOT EXPRESS OPINION</u>

In charging the jury, the court may not express its opinion regarding the evidence.

V.   MOTIONS

A motion is an application to a court in order to obtain an order directing an act to be done. A motion may be made orally or in writing.

A.   Pretrial Motions

★★   1)   MOTION TO DISMISS

After a party is served with a complaint, instead of serving an answer, the party may file a motion to dismiss pursuant to Rule 12(b). A Rule 12(b) motion attacks the *sufficiency of a pleading*, usually a complaint or other claim (e.g., counterclaim, cross-claim). If the court grants a Rule 12(b) motion, the case may be dismissed.

a)   Effect of Dismissal without Prejudice, or with Prejudice

Often, a Rule 12(b) motion dismissal is made *without prejudice*, which means that a plaintiff may re-file its complaint within a limited time period after modification in order to avoid another dismissal on the same grounds. Under certain circumstances, a dismissal may be made *with prejudice*, meaning that the plaintiff is entirely precluded from re-filing a revised complaint against the defendant.

★★   b)   Defenses Appropriate for Rule 12(b) Motions

A party filing a motion to dismiss a pleading pursuant to Rule 12(b) may assert multiple defenses. Some defenses are waived if not asserted in the first responsive motion or pleading. Other defenses are not waivable; they can be asserted at any time.

★★   (1)   Waivable Defenses

(a)   Lack of Personal Jurisdiction

A party may move to dismiss an action alleging that the court lacks personal jurisdiction over the party.

(b)   Improper Venue

A party may move to dismiss a claim alleging that the case is filed in an improper venue.

(c)   Insufficient Process

A party may move to dismiss an action on the ground that the process served on the party was insufficient.

(d)   Insufficient Service of Process

A party may move to dismiss an action on the ground that service of process was insufficient.

★★   (2)   Non-Waivable Defenses

(a)   Lack of Subject-Matter Jurisdiction

A party may move to dismiss an action on the ground that the court lacks subject-matter jurisdiction over the action. Lack of subject-matter jurisdiction may never be waived as a defense; it may be asserted at any time.

(b)   Failure to State a Claim

A party may move to dismiss an action on the ground that the party bringing an action has failed to state a claim. To survive a motion to dismiss for failure to state a claim, a pleading must state a *plausible* claim for relief premised on a defendant's misconduct and not merely on the possibility that the defendant engaged in misconduct.

The defense of failure to state a claim is generally not waived if it is not asserted in a Rule 12 motion or in the defendant's answer. In fact, it may be raised in *any* pleading permitted or ordered, by motion for judgment on the pleadings, or at trial.

(1)   Determining Plausibility of Claim

A federal court takes two steps when determining plausibility of a claim. First, the court identifies the legal conclusions and the factual allegations. The court must accept the well-pleaded factual allegations as true, but need not accept the legal conclusions as true. Second, the court determines whether the complaint states a *plausible* claim for relief based on the factual allegations. The court will make a context-specific analysis of whether a claim for relief is plausible based on the court's common sense and judicial experience. A claim is plausible when the plaintiff pleads enough facts to permit the court to reasonably infer that the defendant is liable for the alleged misconduct. The complaint must state more than a mere possibility that the defendant did not act lawfully.

For example, a court will grant a motion to dismiss for failure to state a claim if the plaintiff alleges enough facts of misconduct by the defendant to support a possible claim for relief, but not enough to support a plausible claim for relief.

(c)   Failure to Join an Indispensable Party

The defense of failure to join an indispensable party is also not waived as a defense if it is not asserted in a Rule 12 motion or in the defendant's answer. Like the defense of failure to state a claim, it may be raised in *any* pleading permitted or ordered, by motion for judgment on the pleadings, or at trial.

★★★   c)   Waiver of Defenses

A party may waive some of the above defenses if the waivable defense is: 1) not asserted in a responsive pleading (e.g., an answer); or 2) not raised in a Rule 12(b) motion to dismiss.

Rule 12(b) provides that:

> Every defense to a claim for relief in any pleading must be asserted in the responsive pleading if one is required. But a party may assert the following defenses by motion: (1) lack of subject-matter jurisdiction; (2) lack of personal jurisdiction; (3) improper venue; (4) insufficient process; (5) insufficient service of process; (6) failure to state a claim upon which relief can be granted; and (7) failure to join a party under Rule 19. *A motion asserting any of these defenses must be made before pleading if a responsive pleading is allowed.* If a pleading sets out a claim for relief that does not require a responsive pleading, an opposing party may assert at trial any defense to that claim. No defense or objection is waived by joining it with one or more other defenses or objections in a responsive pleading or in a motion.

2)   MOTIONS ADDRESSED TO FACE OF PLEADINGS

a)   Motion for a More Definite Statement

A party may file a motion for a more definite statement if served with a pleading that is vague, ambiguous, or unclear, that the party cannot understand or respond to it. A motion for a more definite statement requests that court require the filing of a revised pleading that is sufficiently clear and definitive.

b)   Motion to Strike

A party may move to strike redundant, immaterial, impertinent, or scandalous matters in a pleading. Fed. R. Civ. P. 12(f). If a court grants the motion, any such matter will be excluded from the record.

★   c)   Motion for Judgment on the Pleadings

A motion for judgment on the pleadings under Rule 12(c) is similar to a motion to dismiss under Rule 12(b). What distinguishes a Rule 12(c) motion from a Rule 12(b) motion is that a motion for judgment on the pleadings must be filed *after* the pleadings are closed. When deciding a motion for judgment on the pleadings, a court will determine whether, on the face of all pleadings, the movant is entitled to judgment.

Rule 12(c)-(d) provides that:

> After the pleadings are closed -- but early enough not to delay trial -- a party may move for judgment on the pleadings. If, on a motion . . . [for judgment on the

pleadings or a motion to dismiss for failure to state a claim upon which relief can be granted], matters outside the pleadings are presented to and not excluded by the court, the motion must be treated as one for summary judgment under Rule 56. All parties must be given a reasonable opportunity to present all the material that is pertinent to the motion.

If a motion to dismiss or a motion for judgment on the pleadings includes new or additional matters that are outside of the existing pleadings' contents, a court will usually treat the motion as a motion for summary judgment.

★★★   3)   MOTION FOR SUMMARY JUDGMENT

A party may move for summary judgment to obtain a judicial judgment and avoid a trial. Any party to a claim (e.g., plaintiff or defendant), may move for summary judgment.

★★★   a)   Legal Standard

A motion for summary judgment may be granted if the movant shows that *no genuine dispute exists as to any material fact in the case*, and the movant is entitled to a judgment as a matter of law. Fed. R. Civ. P. 56(a). A motion for summary judgment may be granted if the facts that cannot be genuinely disputed, can only lead to a decision in favor of the movant. If the non-movant cannot win at trial, then the court may grant the motion for summary judgment.

                        (1)   Genuine Issue

An issue of fact is "genuine" if a reasonable jury could return a verdict for the nonmoving party based on the evidence presented by the nonmoving party. If a genuine issue of a material fact exists, the movant cannot prevail.

                        (2)   Material Fact

A fact is "material" if it is relevant to an element of a claim or defense, and its existence would affect the outcome of the case.

                        (3)   All Inferences in Favor of Motion Opponent

When considering the evidence, a court must draw all inferences in favor of the party opposing the motion for summary judgment.

★   b)   Procedure

A party submits a motion for summary judgment and supporting documents.

                        (1)   Supporting Factual Positions

A party may assert that a material fact can or cannot be genuinely disputed. Fed. R. Civ. P. 56(c)(1). A party must support its assertion by citing to specific portions of materials in the record. Fed. R. Civ. P. 56(c)(1)(A). These materials may include documents, declarations or affidavits, depositions, stipulations, interrogatory answers, admissions, or electronically stored information. *Id.*

When a party moves for summary judgment on an issue that it has the burden of persuasion at trial, the party must support its motion with credible evidence that would entitle it to a directed verdict if not controverted at trial.

Alternatively, a party must support its assertion by showing that the materials cited fail to prove the presence or absence of a genuine dispute, or that an adverse party cannot produce admissible evidence to support the fact. Fed. R. Civ. P. 56(c)(1)(B).

(2)   Objection -- Fact is Not Supported by Admissible Evidence

A party can object that the potential evidence cited as support would not be admissible at trial. Fed. R. Civ. P. 56(c)(2).

(3)   Materials Not Cited

The court must consider the materials cited by the parties, but may also consider other materials in the record. Fed. R. Civ. P. 56(c)(3).

(4)   Declarations or Affidavits

A declaration or affidavit used to oppose or support a motion for summary judgment must:

- be based on personal knowledge of the person (i.e., declarant or affiant);
- state facts that would be admissible in evidence; and
- show that the person is competent to testify on the matters stated.

Fed. R. Civ. P. 56(c)(4).

For example, a party may use an affidavit to support the motion, which may be met by contradicting affidavits raising disputes of fact that are required to be resolved at trial, by a finder of fact. As a practical matter, an affidavit should set forth the facts upon which each claim or defense is based.

c)   Failing to Support or Address Facts

If a party does not support or address an assertion of fact, then the court may:

- provide an opportunity to correctly support or address the fact;
- consider the fact undisputed for the motion's purposes;

- grant summary judgment if the motion and supporting materials (containing the facts deemed undisputed) prove that the movant is entitled to the summary judgment; or
- issue some other proper order.

Fed. R. Civ. P. 56(e).

d)   Judgment

A court may grant or deny the motion for summary judgment. If a court grants a motion for summary judgment, the order may be only partial, with respect to certain claims or defenses, or complete. *Id.*

(1)   Reasons Should be on Record

The court should provide the reasons for granting or denying the motion.

(2)   Court May Establish Fact as Established

If a court does not grant a motion for summary judgment, then the court can issue an order establishing a material fact that is not genuinely in dispute. Fed. R. Civ. P. 56(g). The fact will be established in the case. The fact can include an item of damages or other relief. *Id.*

(3)   When Facts not Available to Nonmovant

If a nonmovant cannot present facts essential to justify its opposition to a motion for summary judgment, the nonmovant may submit an affidavit or declaration specifying the reasons the facts are not available. In response to such a submission, a court may:

- defer considering the motion or deny it;
- allow time to obtain affidavits or declarations or to take discovery; or
- issue any other appropriate order.

For example, if a defendant moves for summary judgment before the plaintiff has had an adequate opportunity for discovery, the plaintiff may submit an affidavit detailing the need for further discovery to avoid judgment for the defendant. The court may defer considering the motion for summary judgment until later in the case.

e)   Timing of Motion

Generally, a party may file a motion for summary judgment until 30 days after the end of discovery, unless:

- the court orders otherwise; or
- a local rule sets a different time to file a motion for summary judgment.

Fed. R. Civ. P. 56(b).

★★ **B. Motion for Judgment as a Matter of Law (formerly Directed Verdict)**

A party may move for judgment as a matter of law on the basis that the evidence is insufficient to support the opponent's position.

1) RULING ON MOTION

a) Legal Standard

The motion should be granted if there is no legally sufficient evidentiary basis for the jury to find in favor of the non-moving party. In other words, the court should only grant this motion if it finds that, based on the evidence presented, there is no way that the jury could find for the opposing party.

b) Court Cannot Substitute Judgment for Jury

Granting this motion is "a performance of the court's duty to assure enforcement of the controlling law and is not an intrusion on any responsibility for factual determinations conferred on the jury by the Seventh Amendment." Fed. R. Civ. P. 50 (Advisory Committee's Notes -- 1991 Amendment).

When deciding this motion, a trial court may not:

- determine the credibility of witnesses;
- weigh the evidence; or
- otherwise replace the jury's view of the evidence with that of its own.

(1) Failure to Introduce Evidence Not Dispositive

If a party does not introduce or contradict evidence regarding a jury issue at trial, the issue remains one for the jury to decide (not the court in response to a motion for judgment as a matter of law).

2) TIMING OF MOTION

a) Before Submission of Case to Jury

A party may move for judgment as a matter of law at any time after the close of the opponent's evidence, and before the case is submitted to the jury.

b) Reserve Renewed Motion

A party must timely move for a judgment as a matter of law to preserve a subsequent renewed motion for judgment as a matter of law (formerly called a judgment notwithstanding the verdict).

The purpose of requiring that an initial motion for judgment as a matter of law be made prior to the submission of the case to the jury:

> is to assure the responding party an opportunity to cure any deficiency in that party's proof that may have been overlooked until called to the party's attention by a late motion for judgment.

(1)   Timing of Renewed Motion

The renewed motion must be made within 28 days of the judgment. The renewed motion may only be granted on grounds asserted in an initial motion (made at any time prior to submission of the case to the jury).

★   **C.   Post-Trial Motions**

A party has three general motion options to obtain relief from an unfavorable judgment.

1)   RENEWED MOTION FOR A JUDGMENT AS A MATTER OF LAW

A renewed motion for judgment as a matter of law *is made after* a judgment is entered. The renewed motion must be made within 28 days of the judgment.

The standard for a renewed motion for judgment as a matter of law is the same as for a motion for judgment as a matter of law, set forth earlier.

★   2)   MOTION FOR A NEW TRIAL

a)   General Considerations

A motion for a new trial must be made within 28 days of the judgment. No pre-verdict motion needs to be made as a prerequisite to making a motion for new trial after a verdict. A motion for new trial can be made as an alternative to a renewed motion for a judgment as a matter of law. A motion for a new trial will be more liberally granted than a motion for a judgment as a matter of law because the motion for a new trial does not result in a final judgment. The party must move for a new trial to preserve the right to appeal a judgment. When a party makes a motion for a new trial, the time for appeal is suspended.

b)   Grounds for a New Trial

In order for a motion for a new trial to be granted, there must be a fundamental error affecting the trial outcome or its fairness such as irregularity, misconduct, new evidence, legal error, inadmissible evidence, instruction error, or excessive damages, etc. 11 Charles Alan Wright and Arthur R. Miller, *Federal Practice and Procedure* § 2805-2806 (3d ed. 2007). A court should grant a new trial motion if it is convinced that the jury has reached a seriously erroneous result or that the verdict is a miscarriage of justice.

Unlike a motion for judgment as a matter of law, a motion for a new trial may be granted even if there is substantial evidence to support the jury's verdict. Unlike a motion for judgment as a matter of law, a trial judge considering a motion for a new trial is free to weigh the evidence, and need not view it in the light most favorable to the verdict winner. *Id.* § 2806. But the judge must honor the jury's wisdom. *Id.* The judge should not grant a new trial on the basis that the jury's verdict is contrary to the weight of the evidence unless the verdict causes a miscarriage of justice. *United States v. Landau,* 155 F.3d 93 (2d Cir. 1998).

> [S]ince the credibility of witnesses is peculiarly for the jury, it is an invasion of the jury's province to grant a new trial merely because the evidence was sharply in conflict.

Latino v. Kaizer, 58 F.3d 310 (7th Cir. 1995).

(1)   Juror Bias

At *voir dire*, prospective jurors are questioned in part to determine their potential bias. A motion for a new trial can be made alleging non-disclosure by a prospective juror during *voir dire*. Even though such a motion usually does not succeed, this motion needs to be granted if disqualification of a juror for cause would have been justified. Wright and Miller, *Federal Practice and Procedure* § 2810; *McCoy v. Goldston,* 652 F.2d 654 (6th Cir. 1981). A trial court can conduct a hearing to ascertain if a prospective juror actually is biased before granting a motion for a new trial. *Olson v. Bradrick,* 645 F. Supp. 645 (D. Conn. 1986).

★   3)   RULE 60 MOTION

A party may make a motion pursuant to Rule 60 to obtain relief from a judgment. Relief will be available if the judgment is a result of a mistake or even excusable fault.

a)   Clerical Mistakes

Clerical mistakes in judgments arising from oversight or omission may be corrected by the court at any time of its own initiative or on motion of any party.

b)   Other Grounds

On motion, the court may relieve a party from a final judgment pursuant to Rule 60 for, among other things, the following:

- mistake, inadvertence, surprise, or excusable neglect;
- newly discovered evidence which by due diligence could not have been discovered in time to move for a new trial;
- fraud, misrepresentation, or other misconduct of an adverse party; or

- any other reason justifying relief from the operation of the judgment.

c)   Timing

A Rule 60 Motion must be made within a reasonable time from judgment. Although no firm rule exists, four months has been considered a reasonable time.

VI.   VERDICTS AND JUDGMENTS

A.   Defaults and Involuntary Dismissals

★★   1)   DEFAULT JUDGMENT

A default judgment is a final judgment in a case entered without a determination on the merits.

a)   Motion for a Default Judgment

The most common default judgment scenario for exam purposes involves a plaintiff obtaining a default judgment when a defendant has failed to timely respond to a claim or otherwise defend a lawsuit.

It is important to understand the difference between the terms "entry of default" and "default judgment," including what actions a judge or the court takes, and what actions a clerk of the court takes, to effectuate them. Obtaining a default judgment is a two-step process. First, the court clerk enters a default. Second, the court (either the clerk or judge) enters a default judgment.

(1)   Entry of Default

If a defendant fails to timely respond to a complaint or otherwise defend in a case, a plaintiff can make an application to the clerk to file an entry of default. The plaintiff must attach an affidavit and any other proof relevant to the defendant's failure to respond to the suit to the application for entry of default. The entry of default is a preliminary step. The clerk examines the docket and papers in the plaintiff's filing to determine if there has been an answer or responsive pleading. The clerk may then enter the default. The entry of default is not a judgment.

(2)   Judgment

Once the plaintiff obtains the default, the plaintiff can apply to the court for a default judgment. There is no default judgment until the court orders it.

(a)   Sum Certain

If the claim is for a sum certain (a definite identifiable amount of money damages), the plaintiff may present an affidavit detailing the sum certain to the clerk, and the clerk can enter a default judgment.

(b)   Hearing on Damages

If the amount demanded is not a sum certain, the plaintiff must apply to the court for a default judgment. There must be a hearing where evidence regarding damages is offered. The hearing can be accomplished in some cases on documentary evidence such as affidavits.

(i)   Notice to Defaulting Party

If the party against whom the default judgment has appeared, the party must be given at least seven days notice for the hearing.

(3)   Setting Aside Default

Under certain circumstances, a party against whom a default or default judgment has been entered may be able to set aside the determination.

(a)   Good Cause and Meritorious Defense

A party may file a motion to set aside a default or default judgment. The court will grant the motion if the movant:

- demonstrates good cause or a reasonable excuse for failure to timely plead or otherwise defend the lawsuit; and
- states ultimate facts in support of a meritorious defense to a default.

An entry of default or default judgment may also be set aside if the judgment would be void because of:

- mistake or excusable neglect;
- new evidence;
- fraud or misrepresentation; or
- satisfaction or release.

The commonly tested ground is that the judgment is void. A judgment may be void if the court lacks jurisdiction.

★   (4)   Preclusive Effect of Default Judgment

A default judgment has a preclusive effect if the court entering the default judgment possesses jurisdiction (subject matter and personal) of the case and the parties. *Sewell v. Merrill Lynch*, 94 F.3d 1514 (11th Cir. 1996); *Orca Yachts LLC v. Mollicam Inc.*, 287 F.3d 316 (4th Cir. 2002). A default judgment entered by a federal court exercising diversity jurisdiction in a state possesses identical preclusive effect as exists under that state's law for a judgment of that state's court, unless the state law is incompatible with federal interests. *Semtek Int'l Inc. v. Lockheed Martin Corp.*, 531 U.S. 497 (2001).

The specific preclusive effect the default judgment should receive varies somewhat between states. *Restatement (Second) of Judgments* § 22 and comments. (1982). However, in most states a default judgment precludes a losing party from raising defenses that could have been asserted in the lawsuit, or from making claims that were subject to a compulsory counterclaim requirement of law in that lawsuit. 3 *Moore's Federal Practice* § 13.14 (3d ed.). The defaulting party may challenge the jurisdiction of the court entering the default in the court where the judgment-creditor attempts to enforce the judgment.

(5) Judgment against the United States

A court will only enter a default judgment against the United States (including officers or agencies), if the moving party establishes a claim to relief upon satisfactory evidence.

b) Default as Sanction

A federal court has the authority to sanction a litigant for a violation of the Rules. The most extreme sanction is entering a default judgment. For example, a court may enter a default judgment against a party who refuses to comply with critical discovery orders or fails to attend mandatory conferences. However, a default judgment as a sanction should only be entered in the most extreme circumstances.

(1) Standard of Review

A party's appeal challenging a sanction of default judgment will be reviewed under an abuse of discretion standard. The court examines the severity of the sanction and surrounding circumstances, and may grant the appeal if the trial judge abused his discretion in entering the default judgment.

2) INVOLUNTARY DISMISSAL OF CLAIM

A court has the inherent power to act *sua sponte* (on its own accord), or on motion by a party, to dismiss an action for various reasons.

a) Lack of Prosecution

A court may dismiss an action for lack of prosecution. Lack of prosecution refers to a lack of record activity for an extended period of time. Inactivity by the plaintiff alone may, under the circumstances of the case, justify dismissal. For example, a plaintiff who fails to file any documents or conduct any activity in a case for over two years may have the case dismissed for lack of prosecution.

b) Violation of the Rules

A court may dismiss an action for failure of the plaintiff to comply with the rules of the court or any order of court.

c)   Adjudication on Merits

Unless it states otherwise, an involuntary dismissal order acts as an adjudication on the merits.

d)   Dismissal is a Drastic Remedy

Dismissal is a drastic sanction. It is to be applied only in extreme situations. A court should exercise this right sparingly and only in the face of a clear record of delay or contumacious conduct by the plaintiff. Dismissal may be appropriate when other less drastic sanctions have proven unavailing.

B.   Jury Verdicts -- Types and Challenges

★   1)   NUMBER OF JURORS AND VERDICT

A minimum of 6 and a maximum of 12 jurors must participate in a verdict. Unless the parties otherwise stipulate, 1) a verdict must be unanimous, and 2) no verdict will be taken from a jury that is reduced in size to fewer than 6 members. Fed. R. Civ. P. 48(b).

2)   TYPES OF JURY VERDICTS

a)   General Verdict

Generally, jury determinations are made by general verdict (e.g., liable or not liable).

b)   Special Verdict

In particularly complex cases, the court may require a jury to return a "special verdict" in the form of a special written finding upon each issue of fact. Fed. R. Civ. P. 49(a)(1). Special verdicts are generally disfavored in simple cases.

(1)   Issue Not Submitted to Jury

Unless a party demands that an issue of fact raised by the evidence or pleadings is submitted to the jury, the party waives the right to a jury trial on the issue. Fed. R. Civ. P. 49(a)(3). The party must make the demand before the jury retires.

c)   Written Questions (Interrogatories)

The use of written questions or interrogatories in conjunction with a general verdict affords the court a midpoint between the traditionally favored general verdict and the disfavored special verdict. It is intended to be an improvement on the general verdict, by directing the attention of the jury to the important fact issues, and exposing errors in the deliberative process. Fed. R. Civ. P. 49(b)(1). The jury provides written answers to the written questions.

(1)   Answers Consistent with Verdict

If the general verdict and the written answers are consistent, then the court must approve a judgment based on them. Fed. R. Civ. P. 49(b)(2).

> (2)   Answers Inconsistent with Verdict

If the written answers are consistent but at least one of them is inconsistent with the general verdict, then the court may:

- approve a judgment based on the answers;
- require the jury to further consider the answers and verdict; or
- order a new trial.

Fed. R. Civ. P. 49(b)(3).

> (3)   Inconsistent Answers that Are Inconsistent with Verdict

If the written answers are inconsistent and at least one of them is inconsistent with the general verdict, then the court must:

- not enter a judgment; and
- require the jury to further consider the answers and verdict; or
- order a new trial.

Fed. R. Civ. P. 49(b)(4).

> 3)   CHALLENGE TO JURY VERDICT

> a)   Post-trial Motion Challenging Jury Verdict

As this outline addresses earlier, a party may challenge a jury verdict by making:

- a renewed motion for a judgment as a matter of law;
- a motion for relief from judgment; or
- a motion for a new trial.

> (1)   Motion to Alter or Amend Judgment

A party making a motion to alter or amend a judgment must file the motion within 28 days after entry of the judgment. Fed. R. Civ. P. 59(e). The same time limit applies to a motion for a new trial. Fed. R. Civ. P. 59(b).

> b)   Remittitur (Alternative to Granting New Trial)

If a court believes that a verdict is so excessive that a new trial should be granted for that reason only, it may recommend to the parties that they accept a remittitur. *Remittitur* is the reduction of an award for damages. *Remittitur* can be entered only with the consent of the party awarded damages. It is to be entered only if the amount of the excess can be separately and fairly ascertained.

(1)   Additur of Punitive Damages Not Permitted

Additur is the converse to *remittitur*. *Additur* is the increase of an award for damages that are inadequate. *Additur* may undercut the right to a trial by jury. It is not permitted in the federal court system.

c)   Separate Action Seeking to Set Aside Judgment

A party may bring a traditional action in equity seeking relief of setting aside the judgment that is void or obtained by fraud. Fed. R. Civ. P. 60(d).

★★   **C.   Judicial Findings and Conclusions**

A judge makes findings of fact and conclusions of law when exercising judicial duties. In a jury trial, the *jury is the finder of fact* and the *judge decides the questions of law*. In a bench trial, the judge is both the finder of fact and decides the questions of law.

1)   FINDINGS OF FACT AND CONCLUSIONS OF LAW

When entering an order, a judge may make findings of fact and set forth conclusions of law. The judge must set forth findings of fact separately from conclusions of law.

a)   Judicial Determinations

(1)   Bench Trial

In a bench trial, a judge must set forth the findings of fact separately from conclusions of law. They must be made on the record in order to preserve issues for appeal. The judge may either present them in a written decision or, state them on the record, after the close of the evidence. Fed. R. Civ. P. 52(a)(1).

(2)   Non-Final Injunctions

As in the case of a bench trial, a judge must set forth the findings of fact and conclusions of law that support the judge's determination regarding an interlocutory injunction (e.g., preliminary injunction or temporary restraining order). Fed. R. Civ. P. 52(a)(2).

(3)   Motions

A judge is not required to set forth findings of fact or conclusions of law when ruling on any motion unless they are specifically required by the Rule for the motion. Fed. R. Civ. P. 52(a)(3).

For example, an order granting a motion to dismiss, or a motion for summary judgment, does not need to contain conclusions of law.

b)   Judgment on Partial Findings

If a judge has fully heard a party on an issue and the judge finds against the party on the issue, then the judge may enter a judgment against the party on a claim or defense that can be raised or defeated only with a favorable finding of fact on that issue. Fed. R. Civ. P. 52(c).

c)   Questioning Evidence and Findings

A party may question the sufficiency of the evidence supporting a finding of fact. Fed. R. Civ. P. 52(a)(5). On a party's motion filed within 28 days after entry of a judgment, a trial court may amend its findings of fact, make additional findings, and may amend the judgment accordingly. Fed. R. Civ. P. 52(b).

d)   Clearly Erroneous Standard on Appeal

An appeals court will only set aside a judicial finding of fact if it is clearly erroneous.

★★
D.   Effect; Claim and Issue Preclusion

★★
1)   RES JUDICATA

Res judicata is a general term that refers to all of the different ways in which a prior judgment or determination could have a binding effect on subsequent litigants. It includes both the concepts of claim preclusion and issue preclusion. Claim preclusion prevents a party from litigating an entire claim or any issue which could have been litigated in the prior adjudication of any claim. In contrast, issue preclusion only precludes the re-litigation of a single issue that was actually litigated and determined.

a)   Claim Preclusion

The doctrine of claim preclusion forbids re-litigating entire claims, which were, or could have been, litigated in prior actions. The modern view regarding the scope of a "claim" is that it includes all of the party's rights to remedies against the other party with respect to the same transaction from which the action arose.

For claim preclusion to apply, the following requirements must be met:

- Same parties must exist in both lawsuits;
- The prior judgment must have been rendered by a court of competent jurisdiction;
- A final judgment on the merits must exist; and
- The same cause of action must be involved in both cases.

(1)   Same Cause of Action

The most easily tested prong of the claim preclusion test is the fourth one. In order to determine whether the same cause of action is involved in both lawsuits, courts generally use the *same transaction test*. The test provides that if a claim arose from the same transaction, it is deemed a part of the same cause of action.

Specifically, in order for *res judicata* to apply to a plaintiff's second action:

- the first action must have been decided on the merits;
- the matter contested in the second action must have been (or could have been) resolved in the first action; and
- both actions involve the same parties or their privies.

Sewell v. Clean Cut Mgmt., 463 Mich. 569, 575 (2001).

Many courts apply *res judicata* broadly to bar not only claims already litigated, but also every claim arising from the same transaction that the parties, exercising reasonable diligence, could have raised but did not. *Id.*

(2)   Same Parties

Because of deep-rooted traditions that everyone is entitled to a day in court, a person is not bound by a judgment in litigation in which he was not a party, unless an exception to this general rule applies, including the following:

★★ - a non-party is in sufficient privity with the party. An employer-employee relationship is sufficient to establish privity but a close family relationship alone is not sufficient to establish privity;
- the non-party consents to be bound;
- the non-party is in a pre-existing substantive legal relationship with a party (e.g., preceding and succeeding property owners;
- the non-party assumed control of the prior litigation;
- the non-party seeks to re-litigate through a proxy; or
- a special statutory scheme seeks to foreclose successive litigation by non-parties.

b)   Issue Preclusion (Collateral Estoppel)

The doctrine of collateral estoppel, or issue preclusion, generally prevents a party from re-litigating issues (as opposed to entire claims), that have been previously litigated and determined in a prior action. Issue preclusion applies regardless of whether a second action includes a new claim or cause of action.

(1)   Traditional Approach

The traditional requirements for asserting collateral estoppel are:

- a valid and final judgment was rendered in a prior action;
- an issue of fact was actually litigated, determined, and essential to the judgment in the prior action;
- the same issue arises in a subsequent action; and
- mutuality, meaning the same parties are litigants in both actions.

(2)   Modern Approach

The modern approach to issue preclusion *eliminates the fourth element of mutuality*. Pursuant to the modern approach, a party who is precluded from re-litigating an issue with an opposing party, is also precluded from doing so with another person *unless* he lacked a full and fair opportunity to litigate the issue in the first action, or other circumstances justify affording him an opportunity to re-litigate the issue. Accordingly, when the modern approach is followed, there is a new fourth element in place of the "same parties" requirement that is set forth above. The new fourth element is that the party to be precluded had a *full and fair opportunity* to litigate the same issue in the prior action.

The United States Supreme Court has concluded that trial courts should have broad discretion to determine whether a plaintiff can invoke non-mutual issue preclusion. In one case, the Supreme Court suggested that issue preclusion may not be fair if the plaintiff in the second action could have easily joined in the first action. Prohibiting the application of non-mutual issue preclusion under these circumstances promotes judicial efficiency and encourages plaintiffs to join prior actions rather than waiting to bring the second suit, and effectively gaining two opportunities to litigate the same issue.

VII.   APPEALABILITY AND REVIEW

A.   Availability of Interlocutory Review

As a general rule, an interlocutory order is not appealable. An interlocutory order is an order in a case that does not dispose of the case. For example, a ruling on the admissibility of a piece of evidence is an interlocutory order.

1)   APPEAL IN SPECIFIED TYPES OF CASES

A party may appeal, as a matter of right, an interlocutory order or decree that:

- grants, continues, modifies, refuses, or dissolves an injunction;
- appoints a receiver, or refuses to wind-up a receivership or take steps to accomplish its purpose(s);
- determines the liabilities and rights of the parties to an admiralty case; or
- is final in a patent infringement action, except for an accounting.

28 U.S.C. § 1292(a), (c).

2)   CERTIFICATION OF QUESTION OF LAW

A trial court may certify a non-appealable interlocutory order to an appellate court if:

- the order involves a controlling question of law;
- there is substantial ground for a difference of opinion; and
- an immediate appeal may materially advance the ultimate termination of the litigation.

The judge would include the statement of certification in the order. A party has ten days to appeal the order. The appellate court decides whether to hear the appeal. 28 U.S.C. § 1292(b).

3) WRIT OF MANDAMUS OR PROHIBITION

A trial court's action can also be reviewed by writ of *mandamus* or prohibition. 28 U.S.C. § 1651(a). These extraordinary and drastic remedies may only be invoked when other remedies are not available. *Kerr v. United States,* 426 U.S. 394 (1976) (writ of *mandamus*).

An appellate court may use *mandamus*:

> to prevent a district court from acting beyond its [subject-matter] jurisdiction, or to compel it to take action that it lacks the power to withhold.

Charles Alan Wright et al., 16 *Federal Practice and Procedure* § 3932 (2d ed.).

An appellate court may use a writ of prohibition to *forbid* a lower federal court from taking some action.

★★ B. Final Judgment Rule

1) ONLY FINAL JUDGMENTS ARE APPEALABLE

As a general rule, an appeal can only be taken from a *final judgment*. A final judgment is a dispositive and controlling order that "ends the litigation on the merits and leaves nothing for the court to do but execute on the judgment." *Catlin v. United States,* 324 U.S. 229 (1945).

An appeal from most pre-trial orders is considered *interlocutory* and not appealable as a final decision under the final judgment rule. An interlocutory order may, however, be subject to a collateral attack.

a) Court May Sever Multi-Party or Multi-Claim Judgments

In a case that involves multiple claims or parties, a court may direct entry of a final judgment as to specific claims or parties (less than all), making a final judgment on the severed claim appealable. The court may sever the claims for appeal if it finds no just reason for delay. Fed. R. Civ. P. 54(b). If the trial court does not sever a judgment, the claim will not be subject to appeal until entry of a final judgment in the case.

★★   2)   COLLATERAL ORDER EXCEPTION

The United States Supreme Court has held that the determination of some questions that are collateral to other rights which are asserted in an action may be too important to be deferred for appellate review until after the whole case is adjudicated.

The small category of interlocutory orders that are appealable as collateral orders must satisfy three criteria:

- the court's order must finally dispose of a disputed question;
- the question must be completely collateral to the cause of action; and
- the order that relates to the question must involve an important right that would be "lost, probably irreparably," if review of the question had to wait until after a final judgment occurred.

Cohen v. Beneficial Indus. Loan Corp., 337 U.S. 541 (1949).

"To come within the small class of decisions excepted from the final judgment rule by *Cohen*, the order must conclusively determine the disputed question, resolve an important issue completely separate from the merits of the action, and be effectively unreviewable on appeal from a final judgment." *Coopers & Lybrand v. Livesay,* 437 U.S. 463 (1978).

★★   **C.   Scope of Review for Judge and Jury**

An appellate court can only review matters presented on the trial record. A party must take steps to present matters in order to preserve trial error for appeal.

★★   1)   PRESERVATION OF ERROR

                    a)   Contemporaneous Objection and Offer of Proof

Generally, a party must object to a ruling of a court that the objecting party considers erroneous in order to preserve the matter for appeal.

The objection must be made:

- contemporaneously to the ruling; and
- with particularity regarding the grounds for the objection.

If an objection to the admissibility of evidence is sustained, the non-objecting party is prevented from introducing that evidence at trial. Consequently, in order to challenge the ruling on appeal, the non-objecting party must make an offer of proof that demonstrates what the purported evidence was intended to prove. If the party makes the timely and specific objection, then the party may present an appellate argument in support of the admissibility of the evidence.

(1)   Plain Error Exception – Objection Is Not Required

Plain error is a flaw in the trial process that is so obvious that a failure of the parties or the court to notice and rectify it would seriously affect the fairness or integrity of the judicial proceedings.

To rise to the level of plain error, an asserted error must:

- seriously affect a party's substantial rights; and
- cause an unfair prejudicial impact on the jury's deliberations.

The plain error exception to the contemporaneous objection rule is to be used sparingly, in only those circumstances in which a miscarriage of justice would otherwise result.

b)   Harmless Error Rule

The harmless error rule provides that any error which does not affect the substantive rights of the parties cannot be the grounds for an appeal. Generally, the standard in a civil case is whether an erroneous charge of the jury or ruling of the court would likely have affected a trial's result.

★★   2)   STANDARDS OF REVIEW

An appellate court employs different standards of review for different types of review.

a)   De Novo

An appellate court review of a trial court's determination of a pure issue of law is reviewed using a *de novo* standard. A court reviewing an issue of law under a *de novo* standard provides no deference to the trial court's determination.

b)   Abuse of Discretion

A determination of the admissibility of evidence is reviewed using an abuse-of-discretion standard. A court reviewing an issue under an abuse-of-discretion standard provides deference to the trial court's decision.

c)   Clearly Erroneous

An appellate court reviewing a trial court's finding of fact in a bench trial uses the clearly erroneous standard. An appellate court reviewing a trial court's finding of fact must be significantly deferential to the lower court. The determination should only be reversed if there is a definite and firm conviction that a mistake has been committed. In other words, if the trial court's finding is plausible, the appellate court will not reverse it.

Made in the USA
Middletown, DE
15 October 2015